METHOD

handwritten: 1/05

Berklee Practice Method
TROMBONE
Get Your Band Together

JEFF GALINDO
and the
Berklee Faculty

Berklee Media
Associate Vice President: Dave Kusek
Director of Content: Debbie Cavalier
Marketing Manager: Ami Bennitt
Business Manager: Jennifer Rassler

Berklee Press
Sr. Writer/Editor: Jonathan Feist
Writer/Editor: Susan Gedutis
Production Manager: Shawn Girsberger

ISBN 0-634-00791-2

1140 Boylston Street
Boston, MA 02215-3693 USA
(617) 747-2146

Visit Berklee Press Online at
www.berkleepress.com

DISTRIBUTED BY

HAL•LEONARD®
CORPORATION
7777 W. BLUEMOUND RD. P.O. BOX 13819
MILWAUKEE, WISCONSIN 53213

Visit Hal Leonard Online at
www.halleonard.com

Berklee Practice Method

DESIGN TEAM

Matt Marvuglio	Curriculum Editor
	Dean of the Professional Performance Division
Jonathan Feist	Series Editor
	Senior Writer/Editor, Berklee Press
Rich Appleman	Chair of the Bass Department
Larry Baione	Chair of the Guitar Department
Jeff Galindo	Assistant Professor of Brass
Matt Glaser	Chair of the String Department
Russell Hoffmann	Assistant Professor of Piano
Charles Lewis	Associate Professor of Brass
Jim Odgren	Academic Advising Coordinator
Tiger Okoshi	Associate Professor of Brass
Bill Pierce	Chair of the Woodwind Department
Tom Plsek	Chair of the Brass Department
Mimi Rabson	Assistant Professor of Violin
John Repucci	Assistant Chair of the Bass Department
Ed Saindon	Assistant Professor of Percussion
Ron Savage	Chair of the Ensemble Department
Casey Scheuerell	Associate Professor of Percussion
Paul Schmeling	Chair of the Piano Department
Jan Shapiro	Chair of the Voice Department

The Band

Rich Appleman, Bass
Larry Baione, Guitar
Jim Odgren, Alto Sax
Jeff Galindo, Trombone
Casey Scheuerell, Drums
Paul Schmeling, Keyboard

Music composed by Matt Marvuglio.
Recording produced and engineered by Rob Jaczko, Chair of the Music Production and
Engineering Department.

Contents

CD Tracks

Basics
    CD 1. Tuning Note B♭

Chapter I. Playing Rock ("Sweet")
    CD 2. "Sweet" Full Band
    CD 3. "Sweet" First Part
    CD 4. "Sweet" Second Part
    CD 5. "Sweet" Call/Response 1
    CD 6. "Sweet" Call/Response 2
    CD 7. "Sweet" You're the Trombone
    CD 8. "Sweet" Call/Response 3
    CD 9. "Sweet" Call/Response 4

Chapter II. Playing Blues ("Do It Now")
    CD 10. "Do It Now" Full Band
    CD 11. "Do It Now" Call/Response 1
    CD 12. "Do It Now" Call/Response 2
    CD 13. "Do It Now" Call/Response 3
    CD 14. "Do It Now" You're the Trombone
    CD 15. "Do It Now" Call/Response 4
    CD 16. "Do It Now" Call/Response 5

Chapter III. Playing Blues Swing ("I Just Wanna Be With You")
    CD 17. "I Just Wanna Be With You" Full Band
    CD 18. "I Just Wanna Be With You" You're the Trombone
    CD 19. "I Just Wanna Be With You" Call/Response 1
    CD 20. "I Just Wanna Be With You" Call/Response 2
    CD 21. "I Just Wanna Be With You" Call/Response 3
    CD 22. "I Just Wanna Be With You" Call/Response 4

Chapter IV. Playing Funk ("Leave Me Alone")
    CD 23. "Leave Me Alone" Full Band
    CD 24. "Leave Me Alone" You're the Trombone
    CD 25. "Leave Me Alone" Funk Hookup 1
    CD 26. "Leave Me Alone" Funk Hookup 2
    CD 27. "Leave Me Alone" Call/Response 1
    CD 28. "Leave Me Alone" Call/Response 2

Chapter V. Playing Light Funk ("Affordable")

Chapter VI. Playing Hard Rock ("Don't Look Down")

Chapter VII. Playing Bossa Nova ("Take Your Time")

Chapter VIII. Playing Stop Time ("Stop It")

Foreword

Berklee College of Music has been training musicians for over fifty years. Our graduates go onto successful careers in the music business, and many have found their way to the very top of the industry, producing hit records, receiving the highest awards, and sharing their music with millions of people.

An important reason why Berklee is so successful is that our curriculum stresses the practical application of musical principles. Our students spend a lot of time playing together in bands. When you play with other musicians, you learn things that are impossible to learn in any other way. Teachers are invaluable, practicing by yourself is critical, but performing in a band is the most valuable experience of all. That's what is so special about this series: it gives you the theory you need, but also prepares you to play in a band.

The goal of the *Berklee Practice Method* is to present some of Berklee's teaching strategies in book and audio form. The chairs of each of our instrumental departments—guitar, bass, keyboard, percussion, woodwind, brass, and string—have gotten together and discussed the best ways to teach you how to play in a band. They teamed with some of our best faculty and produced a set of books with play-along audio tracks that uniquely prepares its readers to play with other musicians.

Students who want to study at Berklee come from a variety of backgrounds. Some have great technique, but have never improvised. Some have incredible ears, but need more work on their reading skills. Some have a very creative, intuitive sense of music, but their technical skills aren't strong enough, yet, to articulate their ideas.

The *Berklee Practice Method* teaches many of these different aspects of musicianship. It is the material that our faculty wishes all Berklee freshmen could master before arriving on our doorstep.

When you work through this book, don't just read it. You've got to play through every example, along with the recording. Better yet, play them with your own band.

Playing music with other people is how you will learn the most. This series will help you master the skills you need to become a creative, expressive, and supportive musician that anyone would want to have in their band.

Gary Burton
Executive Vice President,
Berklee College of Music

Preface

Thank you for choosing the *Berklee Practice Method* for trombone. This book/CD package, developed by the faculty of Berklee College of Music, is part of the *Berklee Practice Method* series—the instrumental method that teaches how to play in a band.

The recording included with this method provides an instant band you can play along with, featuring great players from Berklee's performance faculty. Each tune has exercises and practice tracks that will help prepare you to play it. Rock, blues, and funk are just some of the styles you will perform.

The lessons in this book will guide you through technique that is specific to playing the trombone in a contemporary ensemble. When you play in a band, sometimes you will read music, and sometimes, you will create your own part. You may play the melody or support a soloist. You also have to learn to improvise over chord changes. This is very different than classical playing, and these techniques will be a major part of this method.

This book is intended for trombone players who can read notes and basic rhythms, know the basic positions for most notes, and can play all major scales and some arpeggios. Ideally, it should be studied under the guidance of a private teacher, but trombone players learning on their own will also find it invaluable.

Most important, you will learn the skills you need to play trombone in a band. Play along with the recording, and play with your friends. This series coordinates methods for many different instruments, and all are based on the same tunes, in the same keys. If you know a drummer, a bass player, a guitarist, etc., have them pick up the *Berklee Practice Method* for their own instruments, and then you can jam together.

Work hard, make music, have fun!

Jeff Galindo
Assistant Professor of Brass
Berklee College of Music

Basics

Before you start chapter 1, you should understand the following topics.

PARTS OF A TROMBONE

Keep the slide locked whenever your trombone is not being played. This will prevent the outer section from sliding out accidentally and becoming damaged.

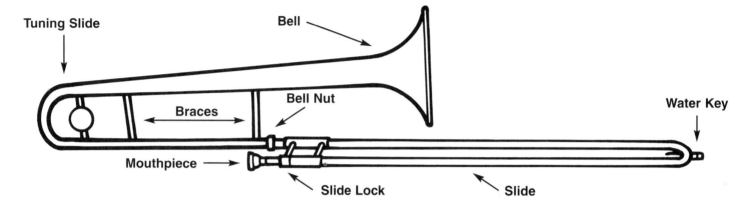

ASSEMBLING THE TROMBONE

The three main sections of the trombone (slide, bell section, and mouthpiece) should be taken apart and reassembled with every use.

1. Secure the slide lock.
2. Fit the bell section onto the slide. Hold the two main sections vertically, the bell 6 inches from the bell opening, and the slide by its two handles (braces).
3. Angle the top of the slide to be two inches from the edge of the bell. When it is in place, secure the bell nut (not too tight!).
4. Fit the mouthpiece in the slide, and gently twist it (not too tight!) so that it stays in place.

To disassemble the trombone, lock the slide, and reverse the steps above. Wipe off every surface with a silver or laquer polishing cloth, and empty the water from your slide. Put the different parts in the proper section of your case—especially the mouthpiece. This keeps them from moving in the case and damaging each other. Once a month, clean your trombone thoroughly, inside and out.

THE SLIDES

Moving the slide should feel almost frictionless. You should use a combination of slide cream (available at most music stores) and water, although some beginners use slide oil. The best thing for the slide is to keep it clean! Special tuning slide grease is available from most music stores.

> **TIP**
>
> If your mouthpiece ever gets stuck in the slide, have a professional repairman remove it. This is inexpensive, and can help you avoid damaging your horn seriously.

HOLDING THE TROMBONE

When you hold a trombone, your left hand supports most of the weight. Your left thumb supports the brace on the bell section. Your left index finger rests on the mouthpiece, and your other fingers hold the inner slide brace.

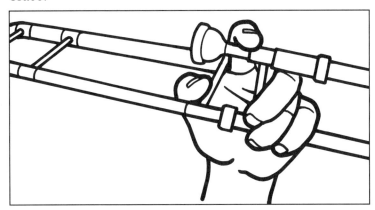

Your right hand holds the outer slide brace.

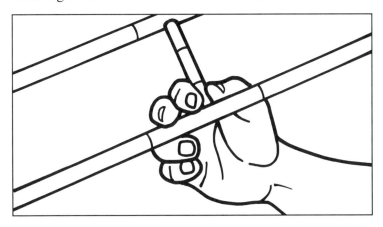

Stand or sit up straight, with your feet firmly on the floor.

Sitting

Standing

EMBOUCHURE

The position of your mouth is called the *embouchure*. Make sure that your mouthpiece is at about the center of your lips. This will give you the best sound and control.

Correct

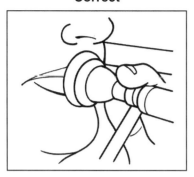

Too Low

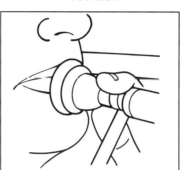

Too High

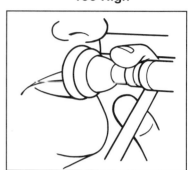

PRACTICE TIP

Good playing technique means more stamina, more facility, and a better sound. You will avoid injuries, which can be painful and even force you to stop playing. If you don't have a teacher, ask an experienced player to review your playing position and make sure that you are on the right track. If it hurts to play, correct your technique right away.

BREATHING

Correct breathing is the most important thing to understand about playing the trombone. Without air, the trombone will not play.

Stand in front of a mirror, put your hand below your rib cage on your abdomen, and breathe. Make sure that your hand is moving and that your chest and shoulders are fairly still, without expanding or rising. Your diaphragm, the breathing muscle, should be doing all the work. This is the correct way to breathe when you play trombone. Practice this every day, before you pick up your horn.

Be relaxed when you breath, and always keep some air in your lungs, without exhaling all the way. This will help you avoid dizziness or even blacking out.

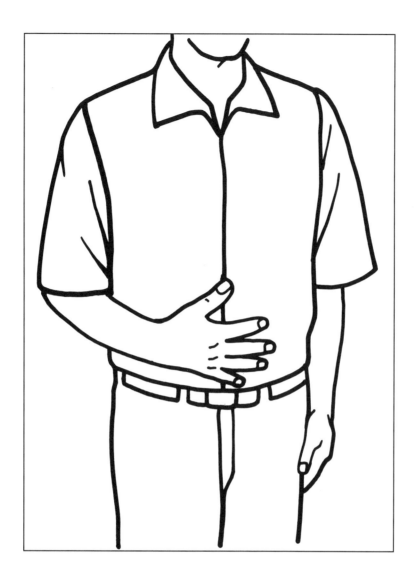

TUNING

LISTEN **1** PLAY

Before you play, tune your trombone to the tuning note on the recording. This will ensure that you are in tune when you play along with the recorded exercises and tunes. Listen to the tuning note on the recording, and then play a B♭. If your pitch is higher than the recorded pitch, pull your tuning slide out from the neck slightly. If your pitch is lower, then push it in slightly. Find the right position for the slide. If you find that the slide has to be too far out for you to play in tune, you may be using too much embouchure pressure.

SLIDE POSITIONS

Here are the slide positions for all the notes used in this method. Other positions are possible, especially if you have an F-attachment. If you find an alternate position easier, you should feel free to use it instead.

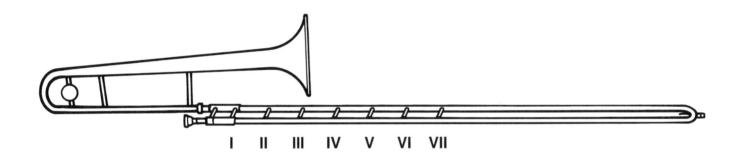

I II III IV V VI VII

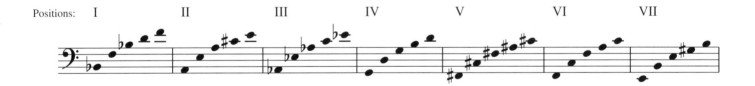

Positions: I II III IV V VI VII

MICROPHONES

If you use a microphone, it should be pointed slightly off center from the bell, about a foot away. To protect your equipment and your ear drums, follow these steps when you plug your mic into an amp or mixing board.

1. Turn off the amp, and set the volume down to 0.
2. Plug your cable into your mic and then into the amp.
3. Turn on the amp.
4. Play at a medium volume. Slowly, turn up the amp volume until it is loud enough.

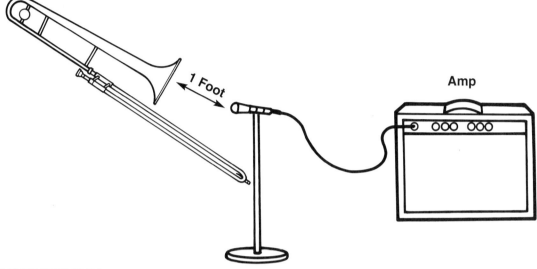

NOTATION

Notes are written on a staff.

Trombone music is written on the "bass clef" staff. Here are the notes for the lines and spaces in bass clef.

Ledger Lines

The staff can be extended with ledger lines.

ACCIDENTALS

Accidentals are symbols appearing before notes, showing that a pitch is raised or lowered for the duration of the measure, unless otherwise indicated.

♭	Flat	Next note down (half step down)
♯	Sharp	Next note up (half step up)
♮	Natural	Cancels a flat or sharp

KEY SIGNATURES

Key signatures indicate a tune's key and show which notes always get sharps or flats. Accidentals on the lines and spaces in the key signature affect those notes throughout the tune unless there is a natural sign. Here are some key signatures used in this book.

| C Major | F Major | G Major | D Major |
| A Minor | D Minor | E Minor | B Minor |

RHYTHMS

Below are the basic rhythms. When there are no actual pitches, as in a rhythm-only exercise, rhythms may be shown on the *percussion clef*. (The beats are numbered below the staff.)

Connect notes using a tie. The first note is held for a total of six beats.

Extend a note's rhythmic value by using a dot. A dot increases the value by one half.

Triplets squeeze three even attacks into the space of two. In this example, the quarter-note beat is divided first into two eighth notes, and then into three eighth-note triplets.

RHYTHMIC NOTATION

Music that just shows rhythms may be written in rhythmic notation. This is common in rhythm exercises, where the emphasis is on rhythm, not on which notes you should play. The stems are the same, but the note-heads are different.

MEASURES

Groups of beats are divided into *measures.* Measure lengths are shown with *time signatures.* This measure is in 4/4 time—there are four beats in the measure, and the quarter note gets the beat.

In 12/8 time, there are twelve beats per measure and the eighth note gets the beat. (Often, 12/8 is felt as four beats, with three lesser beats inside each.)

HOW TO PRACTICE

Organize your practice time into three primary areas: warm-up, technical, and musical. Specific exercises for all three areas are suggested in the Daily Practice Routines section of every chapter. These exercises are based on some of the warm-up sets we use at Berklee. Use them or similar exercises from your teacher, from other books, or that you create yourself.

1. Warm-up. Before you play, always warm up your embouchure. This will help you develop your stamina, improve your sound, and avoid injury, and it will get you ready to play. Warm-up exercises include five areas that you should work on every day: breathing, buzzing, long tones, slurs, and tonguing. 5 to 20 minutes.

2. Technical. Arpeggios, scales, tonguing, slurs, and other exercises will improve your overall agility and range, and also help you warm up further. 25 minutes. Then take a 5-minute break.

3. Musical. Etudes, songs, duets, jam sessions, and materials such as the lessons in this book will help develop your musicality and your ear. 25 minutes.

PRACTICE TIP

When you practice, take a short break every half hour or so. If you practice for more than one hour in a day, break from playing for a couple hours between each hour-long playing session. This will help you avoid injuring your lip by overplaying. To keep your concentration on music during your breaks, spend your time reading, doing ear training exercises, or listening. Just give your lip a break.

Now, let's play!

"Sweet" is a *rock* tune. Rock started in the 1960s and has roots in blues, swing, r&b, and rock 'n' roll. There are many different styles of rock. To hear more rock, listen to artists such as Rage Against the Machine, Melissa Etheridge, Korn, Paula Cole, Bjork, Tori Amos, Primus, Jimi Hendrix, and Led Zeppelin.

LESSON 1
TECHNIQUE/THEORY

Listen to "Sweet" on the recording. The trombone, sax and guitar play the melody together. This tune has two parts. Notice the short introduction before the first part begins.

In the first part of the melody, the trombone plays these notes. Use your ear to find the rhythms.

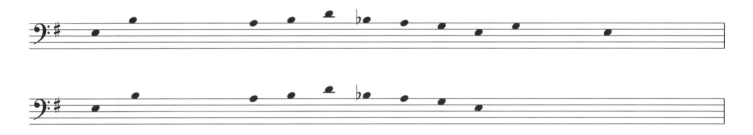

In the second part, the trombone plays these notes.

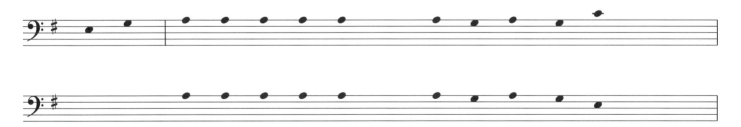

Play along with the recording, and try to match the melody.

1

MELODY

Melodies such as "Sweet" are created out of different *licks*—short, melodic figures or *phrases*. A musical phrase is similar to a phrase in spoken or written language. It is a continuous musical idea that is unbroken and uninterrupted by long rests or periods of silence. Phrases can be short licks, or they can be extended melodies.

In "Sweet," the trombone and lead guitar play the melody, and the other instruments play other kinds of parts. The parts all sound good together because the melody, the *chords* (three or more notes sounded together), and the *groove* (rhythmic time-feel) all work together.

ARTICULATION

Articulation is the way a note is played—short, long, accented, and so on. Choosing good articulations for your notes and phrases will make your melodies come alive.

On a trombone, different articulations are played by changing your breathing and your tonguing. Changing the way you *attack* (start) and *release* (stop) the sound changes the note's articulation.

Legato

Notes in the first part of "Sweet" flow together smoothly. This is *legato* style articulation, often notated with a *slur* marking (⌒). Each note is held for its *full rhythmic value* so that it leads right up to the next note. Only breathe between phrases.

When you attack a legato note, your tongue should move lightly, as if you were saying "dah," touching the back of your top teeth. Each articulation should happen a split second before the note sounds. There should be almost no space between notes.

Practice legato long tones with the recording. Only breathe every two measures, where you see a breath mark (ᕽ). Count in your head while you play (say "and" for "+"). Make sure you hold each note for its full value.

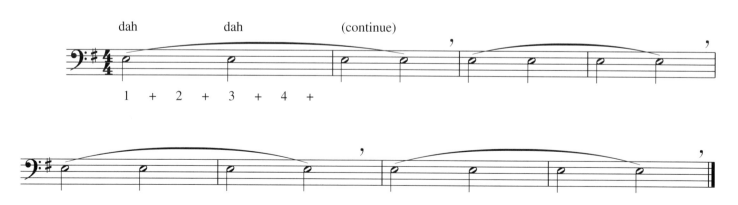

2

Practice the first part of "Sweet" using legato articulation, along with the same track. The notes within each phrase should sound connected.

Staccato

Notes in the second part to "Sweet" are much shorter and more separated. The opposite of legato (long) is *staccato* (short). Staccato notes are indicated with a dot [·]. To play staccato, attack the note with a harder "tah" attack, but then end it quickly, as in the word "tut." The attack is actually a release of the air pressure. The tongue releases the air, with the consonant T starting and stopping the sound.

Staccato notes are not held for their full rhythmic value, and there should be space between notes. Staccato quarter notes are written like this:

The notes sound much shorter than quarter notes—more like sixteenths. Here is the same line written as sixteenth notes. As you can see, the dots are much easier to read than the sixteenth-note flags with dotted eighth-note rests.

Practice staccato articulations with the recording, one note per beat. Only breathe every two measures, where you see a breath mark. Though the notes are short, you should still think about phrasing, and breathe between phrases rather than between notes. Keep your air moving.

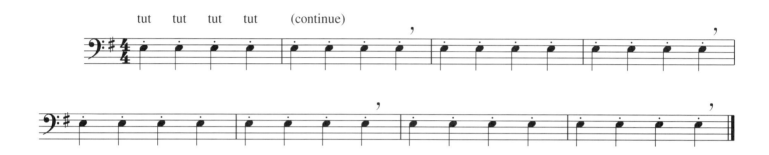

Now practice staccato eighth notes with the recording. Try the E in either octave. Keep using that "tut" syllable.

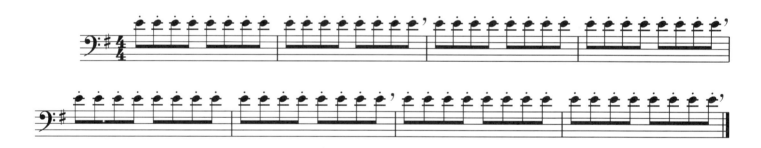

The licks in the second part of "Sweet" each have three notes that are played staccato on the recording. The other notes shouldn't be as short. Practice these licks a few times to get the staccato feel, and then practice the whole section with the recording.

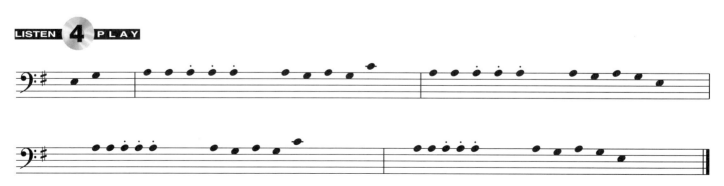

Keep the tip of your tongue behind your top teeth. Playing a combination of staccato and legato notes will make it much easier to play accurate rhythms and stay in the groove.

Other Staccato Articulations

You may see other kinds of staccato articulation marks besides the dot. The *short* accent (^), sometimes called "swing staccato," is shorter duration than a normal note, but not as short as staccato—about a third of the original note's value. Some also use a short accent to mean "louder" or "punched." A short used along with a line (⌄) is longer than a regular short accent—more like half the original note's value.

Another accent that you may see is an accent with a line (≥). This is held for the full duration and played loudly.

LEAD SHEETS

Articulations may be marked in formal, published music. When you play in a band, more often, you will use informal music that only shows chord symbols and melody, usually with no articulations, no phrasing, and no other expressive markings. This is called a *lead sheet*. Finding the right articulations will be up to you.

This is what the first part to "Sweet" looks like on a lead sheet.

The whole band may read the same lead sheet. Each player will use it differently to create a part for their instrument. As a trombone player, one way you will use the lead sheet is to read and play the song's melody.

The piano, guitar, and bass all play parts using notes from the chords. By tuning in to the chords, you'll find it easier to keep your place in the music. When it's your turn to *solo* (improvise), the chord symbols will be useful to you as well, as we will see in later chapters.

Different bands will create different parts for the same tune. This is one of the coolest things about lead-sheet notation: it leaves room for individual interpretation.

You will see the full lead sheet to "Sweet" in lesson 4.

LESSON 2
LEARNING THE GROOVE

WHAT IS A GROOVE?

A *groove* is a combination of musical patterns in which everyone in the band feels and plays to a common pulse. This creates a sense of unity and momentum. The *rhythm section* (usually drums, bass, guitar, and keyboard) lays down the groove's dynamic and rhythmic feel. A singer, trombone player, or other soloist also contributes to the groove, and performs the melody based on this feel.

LISTEN **2** P L A Y

Listen to "Sweet." As is common in hard rock, the groove to "Sweet" has a strong, clear pulse and a loud, forceful sound. The drums play a heavy, repetitive beat. The bass outlines the harmonic structure. The rhythm guitar and keyboard play chords. The trombone and lead guitar play the melody. Everyone uses the same rhythms, though often at different times. This makes the whole band sound like one unit; they're all *hooked up* with the groove.

In lesson 1, when you played along with the recording and matched the trombone part, you hooked up with a groove and became part of the band.

TROMBONE IN A GROOVE

In our band, the trombone player actually has three roles in the groove: melody, improvisation, and accompaniment licks called *backgrounds*, which you will add. If there were several trombone players, there might be another kind of role—that of a member of a trombone section. In a section, the trombones may play chords together, they may all play the same melody in *unison* (at the same time), or they may play group backgrounds. In a smaller band, like the one on our recording, there is only one trombone player. He's "out front," and at the center of attention.

HOOKING UP TO ROCK

As a trombone player, though you are not a member of the rhythm section, you are still part of the groove and must tap into its rhythmic feel. The way that you play should help the other band members feel the beat or pulse you feel.

The way to hook up to a groove is by learning its unique pulse and rhythmic feel. Then, your playing will hook up rhythmically with the rest of the band. Your phrasing and articulation will help you define the rhythms of your part and hook up to the groove.

> **PRACTICE TIP**
>
> When you learn a groove, start by counting out the rhythms, without blowing into your instrument.

Count along with the beat, repeating "1, 2, 3, 4" through every measure. While you count, clap along with the snare drum on the *backbeat*—beats 2 and 4, where you see the circles below. A strong backbeat is one of the characteristics of rock grooves.

While you clap and count, tap your foot on the quarter-note pulse.

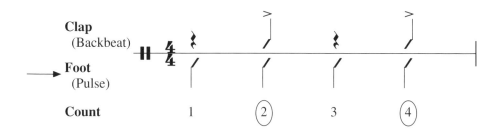

This tune has a sixteenth-note feel, so change your counting to sixteenth notes, matching the cymbals. On each beat, count evenly, "1 e + a, 2 e + a, 3 e + a, 4 e + a" (say "and" for "+"). Try saying this first at a slower tempo, without the recording, until you get the hang of it. When you are ready, play the recording and say the syllables in tempo.

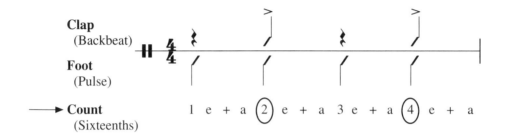

Clap the rhythm of the trombone's first part to "Sweet," and feel the sixteenth-note *subdivisions* (divisions within a beat). When you are ready, tap along with the recording.

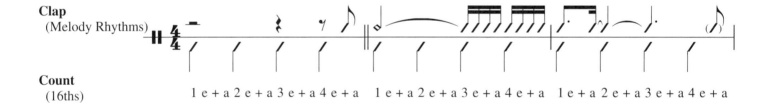

Next, play the notes. Count along in your head. When you are ready, play along with the recording. Use legato articulations, and hook up with the groove. Try to play the whole melody.

Use this approach when you learn any new music, particularly when there are tricky rhythms. Find the pulse and its subdivisions, count out the rhythms, and then play the notes. Hook up with the drums and bass. Try it with the notated part of the second part to "Sweet." Also try it with the background parts coming up later in this lesson.

BACKGROUNDS

When another instrument is playing the melody or soloing, you may support its part by playing background licks, also called "backgrounds." Keep them simple so that they do not distract from the melody. Sometimes, backgrounds will be included in your written part, but often, you will create them yourself.

Play the following background part along with "Sweet." Use it to support the melody and the improvised solo. Notice that the backgrounds only come on the second phrase of each section. They are used here to make the repeated phrases more interesting and to help give the tune a sense of shape. Remember that the first part begins after the introduction.

Finally, play the whole tune, following your ear and not looking at the music. Use different articulations for each part, and hook up with the rhythm section.

DOUBLE THE BASS

Another option, when you are not playing melody, is to double the bass part. This is especially common in rock, where the bass line is such a prominent part of the groove. The bass line to "Sweet" is based on repeated licks. This kind of line is called a *riff*.

When you double the bass, you may simplify the part. This supports the bass line without distracting from it.

Practice the bass part to "Sweet," and then play it along with the recording.

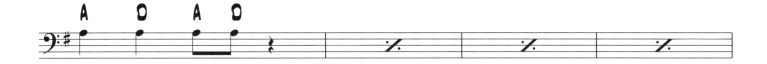

LESSON 3
IMPROVISATION

Improvisation is the invention of music. When you improvise, you tell the story of what you think about the tune and what it means to you. Though an improvised solo or background part may seem spontaneous to the audience, the musician probably did a lot of preparation before performing it. There are three things you must know before you start improvising: the song melody, when you should play, and what notes will sound good.

FORM AND ARRANGEMENT

When you are preparing to improvise on a tune, start by learning how it is organized. This will let you know when you should start your improvisation and where the chords change.

LISTEN 2 PLAY

Listen to "Sweet," and follow the trombone. After an introduction by the rhythm section, the trombone, sax, and guitar play the melody. Then, there is an improvised trombone solo. Finally, the trombone plays the melody again, followed by a short ending.

During the improvised solo, you can still feel the written melody. That's because the improvisation follows the same chords as the written melody. This repeating chord structure is the same throughout the entire tune, and is called the song's *form*—its plan or structure.

A common way to show this organization is with a *chord chart*. Chord charts don't show rhythm or pitch, just measures and chord symbols. The slash marks (/ / / /) mean "play in time."

The chord chart makes it easy to see that the form of "Sweet" is sixteen measures long. It has two primary musical ideas: the first eight measures present the first idea (Idea "A"), with the **E- A E-** patterns. The second eight measures present the second idea (Idea "B"), with the **A- D A- D** patterns. This form can be described simply as "AB" or "AB form." These letters help us remember the form, freeing us from having to read while we're performing.

HEAD/CHORUS

One complete repetition of this form is called a *chorus*. A chorus can feature the written melody, in which case it is called the *head*, or it can feature just the chord structure, supporting an improvisation. (The word *chorus* is also used to mean a song section that is alternated with varying verses. In this book, however, the word "chorus" is only used to mean "once through the form.")

ARRANGING "SWEET"

Your band can choose how many choruses you want to play and create your own *arrangement* of "Sweet." The number of choruses depends on how many players will improvise when you perform the tune. On the recorded performance of "Sweet," one player (the trombone) solos for two choruses. Often, several members of the band will take turns playing choruses of improvised solos. A solo can be one or two choruses, or even more.

On the recording, the same basic arrangement is used for all the tunes: the head, an improvised trombone solo, and then the head again. There are often short introductions and endings as well.

Listen to "Sweet," and follow the arrangement. This is the arrangement for "Sweet" played on the recording:

INTRO	HEAD	SOLO: 2x	HEAD	ENDING
4 MEASURES	1 CHORUS = 16 MEASURES	1 CHORUS = 16 MEASURES	1 CHORUS = 16 MEASURES	2 MEASURES

When you play "Sweet" with your band, you can play your own arrangement, adding extra solo choruses, different endings, or other changes.

IDEAS FOR IMPROVISING

When you improvise, some notes will sound better than others. There are many ways to find notes that will sound good. You can use the notes from the tune's melody, you can use notes from the chords, and you can use notes from scales that match the tune. Eventually, this becomes intuitive, and you can just follow your ear.

SCALES: E MINOR PENTATONIC

The trombone player on this recording of "Sweet" built much of his solo using notes from a *pentatonic scale.* Pentatonic scales are among the simplest and most versatile types of scales in all of music. All pentatonic scales have five notes. There are two common types of pentatonic scales: major and minor. For "Sweet," the soloist used the *minor pentatonic* scale built on E. This scale works well here because the tune is in the key of E minor. Notice that the E is repeated, up an octave, to close the scale.

Use this scale to create your improvised licks. You only need a few notes to create a lick, so divide the scale into halves. Use one half for some licks and the other half for other licks. This will add contrast between them.

Group 1   # Group 2

Here are some of the licks that can be created using some notes from group 1.

Here are some of the licks that can be created using some notes from group 2.

You may have noticed that all of these licks use the same rhythm. This is the rhythm used above.

Plugging different notes into the same rhythm is another good technique for building solos. It makes the licks sound related, like part of the same thing. You don't need to use the same exact rhythm every time, but some repetition can be very effective.

CALL AND RESPONSE

Listen to each phrase, and then play it back, echoing it exactly. Each lick comes from the E minor pentatonic scale, using the groupings and the rhythm discussed above. Slashes ("∕") in measures marked "play" mean that you should play in time during those measures. Listen carefully, and hook up with the groove.

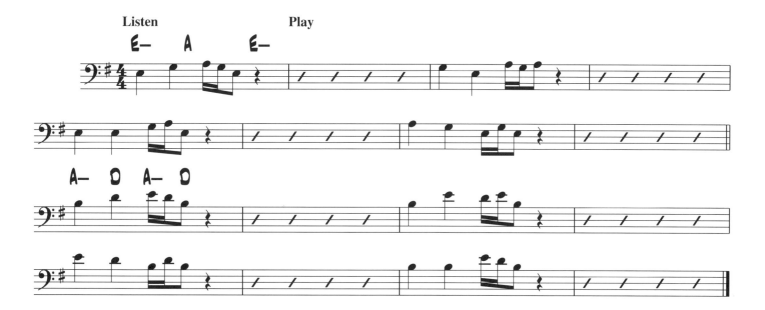

Keep practicing that track until you can echo all phrases perfectly. Then do the same thing for the phrases on this next track.

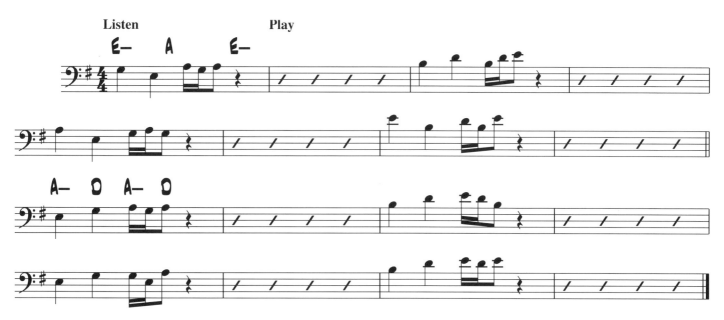

Play the same two tracks again. This time, instead of echoing the phrases exactly, answer them with your own improvised phrases. Use the same rhythms, and only use notes of the E minor pentatonic scale.

Write out some of your own licks, like the ones you have been playing. Don't worry about perfecting your notation; just sketch out your ideas. This will help you remember them when you are improvising.

Create a 1-chorus solo using any techniques you have learned. Memorize your solo, and practice it along with the recording.

PLAY IN A BAND TIP

When playing in a band, listen to the other players' parts and try to create a musical conversation. This makes playing much more fun, and more musical too. When you are improvising a solo, listen to what the other instruments are playing. They will suggest many ideas that you can use in your solo, such as rhythms and licks, and you will inspire each other.

LESSON 4
READING

When you play in a band, sometimes, you will get a trombone part that shows exactly what you should play. Other times, you may get a lead sheet, giving you more freedom to create your own part. You should be able to play from either one.

TROMBONE PART

Below is a written trombone part to "Sweet." This part shows articulation markings and rehearsal letters.

HARD ROCK	Style indication. This tune is hard rock, and you should play it in that style: heavy bass, strong beat, sixteenth-note feel, and other elements typical of that hard-edged sound.
♩ = 86	Metronome marking. This tells you how fast you should play this tune. If you have a metronome, set it to 86, and play "Sweet" at that tempo.
INTRO	Introduction. The written part begins with an introduction, which is made up of four measures of the B section.
3	A bar with a number over it means that you should rest for that number of measures. The introduction begins with just the rhythm section, so you can sit out. But count along, so you are ready to come in on the pickup to letter A.
A	Rehearsal letter. These are different than form letters, which you saw in lesson 3. These letters help you when you are practicing with other musicians because everyone's parts have the same letters marked at the same places.
‖: :‖	Repeat signs. Play the music between these signs twice (or more).
A9	Rehearsal letter with measure number. These mark different areas within a chorus. Again, this can be helpful during rehearsals.

AFTER SOLOS, REPEAT TO ENDING

When the soloists are finished, play the head one more time, and then proceed to the measures marked "Ending."

ENDING	A final section that is added to the form. End the tune with these measures.

Play "Sweet" along with the recording. Follow the trombone part exactly as it is written.

LEAD SHEET

Lead sheets present only the chords and melody, giving you a little more interpretive freedom than full formal trombone parts do. Notice that there is no written introduction on this lead sheet. The introduction you hear in the recording is an interpretation of the lead sheet by that band. Similarly, no backgrounds are included. Your band should create your own unique arrangement, and you should create your own backgrounds.

PLAY IN A BAND TIP

As you rehearse "Sweet," follow the lead sheet. It will help you keep your place in the form.

CHAPTER I
DAILY PRACTICE ROUTINE

WARM-UPS

Begin every practice session by warming up your embouchure. Warming up will make your horn respond much easier, help you avoid injury, and is generally the best thing you can do to improve your playing. Every day, warm up all five areas: breathing, buzzing, long tones, slurs, and tonguing. This chapter gives examples of each type of warm-up exercise. Continually add to these, and vary or replace them as your playing develops. Additional exercises are presented in later chapters. 5 to 20 minutes.

1. **Breathing.** Before you pick up your horn, rest your hand below your rib cage and make sure you are breathing from your diaphragm, not from your chest.

   Inhale steadily over six steady counts with your metronome at 60–72 bpm. Hold it (use your diaphragm, not your throat) for six counts. Then exhale steadily over six steady counts. Repeat this five times. If you feel light-headed, stop and rest.

2. **Buzzing.** Draw (or imagine) a dot on a sheet of paper. Blow on that dot, focusing your air only on the dot, without puffing your cheeks. Then buzz the mouthpiece, keeping the same focus of air. Try to move the paper with your air.

   Listen to the tuning note, play a note on a piano, or just imagine a note. Sing it, then match its pitch by just buzzing the mouthpiece. See how long you can play a strong, steady buzz. Sing and then buzz other pitches.

3. **Long Tones.** Long-tone exercises will get your blood going and will help you develop your sound. When you play, project to the far wall of your room to get a full sound. Play the following warm-up exercises mezzo-forte with your metronome at 60–72 bpm. Breathe only where shown, and watch the enharmonics!

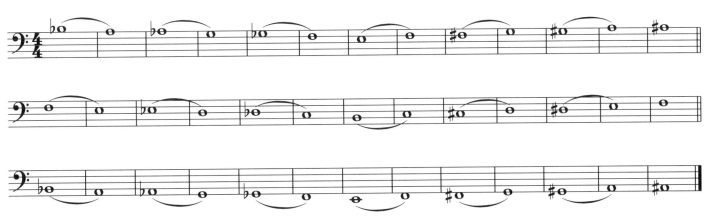

4. Slurs. Tongue only the first note in each position. Make the slurs smooth and even. Once you can play the 2-note slur exercise smoothly and evenly, progress to the 3-note (chapter 2) and then 4-note slurs (chapter 4), when you are ready. Eventually, try to work all three exercises—at the same tempo—into your daily warm-up. Keep the tempo at 60–72 bmp.

5. Articulation

Legato

Practice these two legato exercises along with the recording to the first part of "Sweet." Breathe only where you see the breath marks. The notes should sound almost connected to each other.

PRACTICE TIP

When you begin a legato note, move your tongue as if you were saying "dah." This is softer than "tah," and will sound more legato. At the end of each phrase, imagine that you are saying "hut," seemlessly blending the H of "hut" with the H of "dah." The H will help you sustain your breath support and define the phrase ending.

LISTEN **3** PLAY

Legato Exercise 1

Legato Exercise 2

dah dah dah dah - hut dah dah dah dah - hut

dah dah dah dah - hut dah dah dah dah - hut

Staccato

Your tongue should be at the top of your top teeth when you articulate each note, touching the same place as when you say "tut." For a softer touch, tongue as if you were saying "da." Practice this exercise both ways.

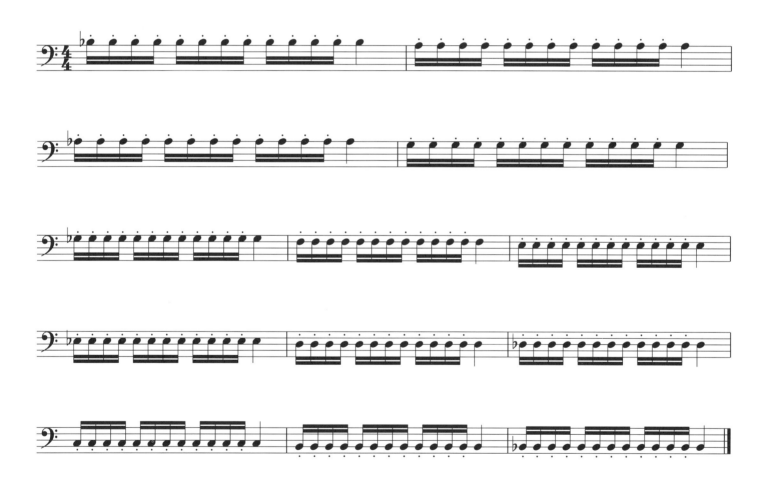

TECHNIQUE

E MINOR PENTATONIC SCALE PRACTICE

Practicing scales will help you develop your reading, your ear, and your general knowledge of music. As an improviser, scales will provide you with notes to use in your solos.

Repeat this exercise five times, reading the music as you play. Then play it five more times from memory.

> **PRACTICE TIP**
>
> Practice a scale in three keys every day. The next day, practice it in three other keys. In four days, you will be able to play the scale in all twelve keys. Then start the cycle again. When you can play that scale from memory in all twelve keys, repeat the process for a different type of scale (major, minor, blues, and so on). Review all the scales you know as part of your practice.

SCALE PRACTICE

Here are the notes of the E minor pentatonic scale through two octaves. When you are comfortable playing all of these notes, you'll be able to use them when you improvise.

This next exercise will help you master the E minor pentatonic scale throughout the trombone's register. Practice it with both legato and staccato phrasing. Breathe only at the breath marks. This exercise is based on the form of "Sweet," so you can practice it along with the track, playing it several times. Begin after the introduction.

"SWEET" SCALE STACCATO EXERCISES

Practice the E minor pentatonic scale along with the recording, using staccato articulations. Listen to the drums, and try to play your notes exactly in time.

"Sweet" Staccato 1

"Sweet" Staccato 2

Create and write out your own exercises based on the E minor pentatonic scale. The more ways you find to make melodies from that scale, the more you make music that's truly your own.

IMPROVISATION PRACTICE

CALL AND RESPONSE

1. Echo each phrase, exactly as you hear it.
2. Improvise an answer to each phrase. Imitate the sound and rhythmic feel of the phrase you hear, and use the notes from the E minor pentatonic scale.

LISTEN **8** PLAY

Keep practicing that track until you can echo all phrases perfectly. Then do the same thing for the phrases on this next track.

RHYTHMIC IMPROVISATION

Practice these rhythmic licks. First sing them, then play them on your instrument using notes from the E pentatonic scale. Spend time with each one, using different note combinations with the same rhythm. Then create your own 2-bar licks, using the rhythms below as one bar and your own rhythm as the other.

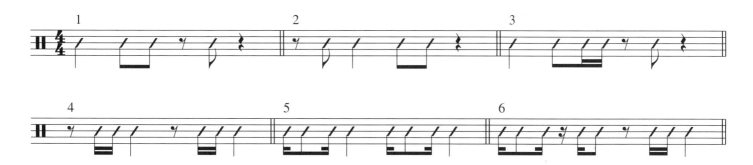

LICKS

Practice and memorize each of these licks. Then create some similar licks of your own. These can be used in a solo or as backgrounds.

SOLO PRACTICE

Practice this solo along with the recording. You may want to use some of these licks in your own solos. Notice that the B-flat is not in the E minor pentatonic scale.

CHALLENGE

Improvise your own solos along with the recording, based on any of the licks you have been playing.
Alternate each written lick with your own improvisation, deciding what to play while you are actually playing.
Play the written lick, then your improvisation, then the same written lick again, then a different improvisation, and so on.

MEMORIZE

Memorizing the licks and melodies from these exercises will help you play the tune, especially when you improvise. What you practice helps you when you perform. But performing is the best practice, so get together with some other musicians and learn these tunes with your own band.

Memorize the trombone part to "Sweet." Also memorize the lead sheet. The "Summary" shows everything you need to play "Sweet" from a lead sheet. Memorizing it will help you memorize the tune.

SUMMARY

PLAY "SWEET" WITH YOUR OWN BAND!

"Do It Now" is a *blues* tune. Blues began in the late 1800s, and it has had a profound influence on American music styles, including rock, jazz, and soul. To hear more blues, listen to B.B. King, the Blues Brothers, Robben Ford, Bonnie Raitt, James Cotton, Albert King, Paul Butterfield, and trombonists J.J. Johnson, Bill Harris, Lawrence Brown, Frank Rosolino, Jimmy Knepper, Benny Green, Roswell Rudd, Carl Fontana, Phil Wilson, and Hal Crook.

LESSON 5
TECHNIQUE/THEORY

LISTEN **10** PLAY

Listen to the recording of "Do It Now," and play along. Try to match the trombone. The melody has three lines. Each starts differently, but ends the same.

First Line

Second Line

Third Line

PRACTICE TIP

In melodies, look for patterns—notes that are the same or similar from one phrase to the next. In "Do It Now," the three phrases end exactly the same. Also, the first two phrases are very similar, with the only difference being that the first A-natural in the first phrase changes to an A-flat in the second. As you learn songs, notice what remains the same and what's different. You'll learn them faster.

BREATHING

When you play a phrase, you need to have enough air (breath) in your lungs for the whole phrase. It should feel as natural to you as saying a complete sentence in one breath. You don't run out of air when you speak, so you shouldn't run out of air when you play!

Inhale before you begin playing. Develop the habit of breathing *during the count-off*, before you begin.

Here's how it works for a tune like "Do It Now." This tune begins on beat 1 of the first measure. During the measure leading up to where you play, exhale during beats 1 and 2, and then inhale during beats 3 and 4.

PRACTICE TIP

A full breath will help you produce a big, full trombone sound.

BREATH MARKS

In chapter 1, you saw the breath mark symbol ( ). Most music won't include these, so you have to write them in yourself. Plan your breathing so that you can play complete phrases without interruption.

Play the first phrase of the melody along with the recording, and only breathe at the marks. Make your breaths even, and don't trim too much time off of the whole notes. Next, try playing through the first mark, and only breathe at the end of the 4-measure phrase.

LISTEN **10** PLAY

When a melody has many long notes, plan your breathing so that you can hold all notes for their full duration. Inhale deeply so that you will have enough air for the end of the phrase. If you are running out of air, try to find an additional place to breathe so that the sound remains strong throughout the phrase.

WRITE IN YOUR OWN BREATH MARKS

Below is the entire melody of "Do It Now." Play through it, and write in your own breath marks. Try to preserve the melody's natural phrases, and be sure you can maintain a strong sound throughout. Practice it along with the recording. Change your markings if you think you can improve them.

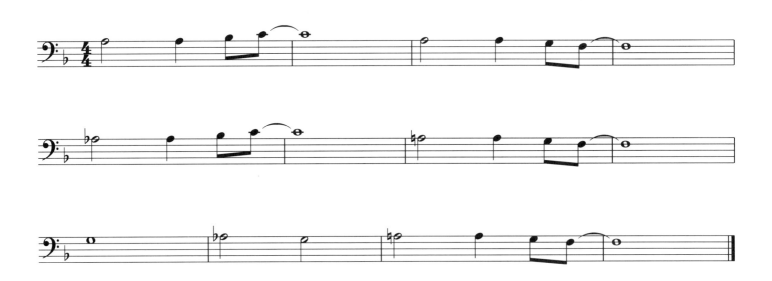

LESSON 6
LEARNING THE GROOVE

HOOKING UP TO A BLUES SHUFFLE

Listen to "Do It Now." This groove has its roots in traditional r&b, gospel, and jazz. The feel is often called a *12/8 shuffle* because of the twelve eighth notes in each bar. (The drums play these on the ride cymbal and hi-hat.)

Tap your foot on every beat, and count triplets: "1 trip-let 2 trip-let 3 trip-let 4 trip-let." The basic pulse (foot) is on the quarter note. However, each pulse also has an underlying triplet that divides the beat into three equal parts:

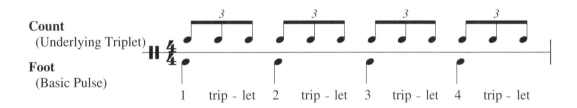

This triplet feel is part of what makes the beat a *shuffle*. While all shuffles don't include triplets on every single beat, the underlying triplet *feel* is always present.

The triplet is a fundamental aspect of all swing and shuffle beats. Understanding and feeling the concept of subdivisions (dividing the pulse into smaller rhythms) will help you play many other kinds of grooves.

"Do It Now" begins with the drums playing two beats of triplets. This establishes the shuffle groove. Listen for the steady triplet beat in the hi-hat, and find the triplet patterns in the other instruments. Listen to the bass part. Which beats have a triplet feel? Is the triplet pattern the same in every measure or does it change?

SWING EIGHTH NOTES

Eighth notes in shuffle grooves are usually played as triplets, even though they are notated as *straight* eighth notes.

Straight   Swing

Though these rhythms look different, in some musical styles, they are played the same. The notated part to "Do It Now" shows eighth notes notated like this:

Since it is a shuffle tune, they are played more like this:

The part is easier to read without the triplet markings on every beat, and the rhythms are played as triplets even though they are notated as if they were regular eighth notes. Interpreting rhythms in this way is called "swinging the eighth notes." Swing eighth notes are common in many styles of music, including blues, jazz, and swing.

Sometimes, the word "swing," "swing feel," or "shuffle" appears on the lead sheet, telling you how to play eighth notes. If there is no such indication, try it both ways and choose which fits the groove best. The style of the tune may help you choose whether to swing your eighth notes or play them straight.

LISTEN **10** PLAY

Listen again to "Do It Now" and play the trombone part along with the recording. Feel the triplets on every beat, listen to the drums, and hook up with the groove.

BACKGROUNDS

Practice this background part along with the recording. Swing your eighth notes!

Create your own background part. When the melody is active, your part should be inactive. Keep it simple so that it supports the soloist's improvisation without interfering with it. Write it out, and practice it with the recording.

LESSON 7
IMPROVISATION

FORM: 12-BAR BLUES

LISTEN 10 PLAY

Listen to "Do It Now," and follow the form. The form of this tune is called a *12-bar blues*.

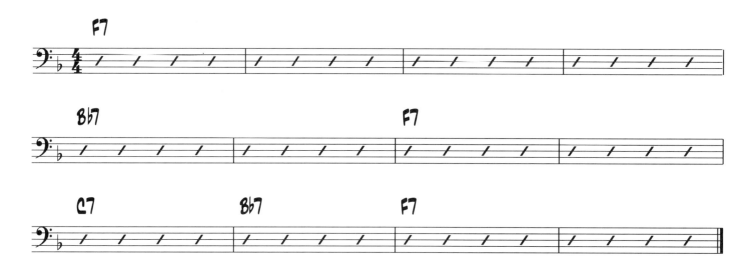

A 12-bar blues has three 4-bar phrases. It is common for the first two phrases in the melody to be similar and the third one to be different. This form is very common in many styles of music, including jazz, rock, and funk.

In "Do It Now," the first phrase has four bars of the I chord (F7). The second phrase has two bars of the IV chord (Bb7) followed by two bars of the I chord (F7). The third section has one bar of V (C7), one bar of IV (Bb7), and then two bars of I (F7). This is typically the way that chords move in blues.

Memorize the blues form and chord progression. You will see it again many times throughout your career.

ARRANGEMENT

"Do It Now" begins with the drum playing two beats of triplets. This is called a *pickup*—a short introduction, less than a measure long, that leads to a strong downbeat. Here is the arrangement played on the recording.

LISTEN **10** PLAY

PICKUP	HEAD: 2x	SOLO: 2x	HEAD	ENDING
2 Beats Drums	‖: 1 Chorus = 12 Measures :‖	‖: 1 Chorus = 12 Measures :‖	1 Chorus = 12 Measures ‖	4 Measures ‖

> **PRACTICE TIP**
>
> When you listen to any music, figure out the arrangement. How long is the head? Is there an introduction or an ending? How many solo choruses does the band take?

SCALES: F BLUES

In chapter 1, you created bass lines using the E minor pentatonic scale. Here is the F minor pentatonic scale:

The *F blues scale* has just one more note—the flat fifth degree (C-flat or B-natural):

Practice the notes of the F blues scale over the range of your trombone. Extend it, if you can.

CALL AND RESPONSE

In these call-and-response exercises, divide the F blues scale into two groups. The B-natural will be used in both groups. The first chorus draws from group 1, and the second chorus draws from group 2. The notes of each group can be played in any octave.

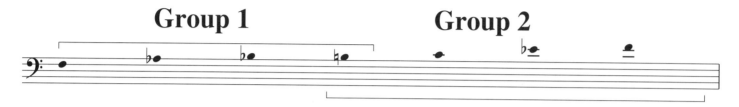

Use this rhythm for each lick.

PRACTICE TIP

Practice call and response exercises by first singing back each phrase, using the syllable "dah." Then play the tracks again, this time with your instrument.

---

1. Echo each lick, exactly as you hear it.
2. Improvise an answer to each lick. Use the same rhythm for each answer, but choose your own notes.

Use notes from group 1 in this chorus.

LISTEN 11 PLAY

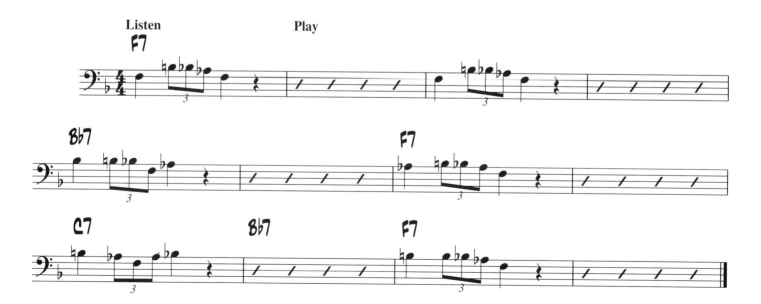

Use notes from group 2 in this chorus.

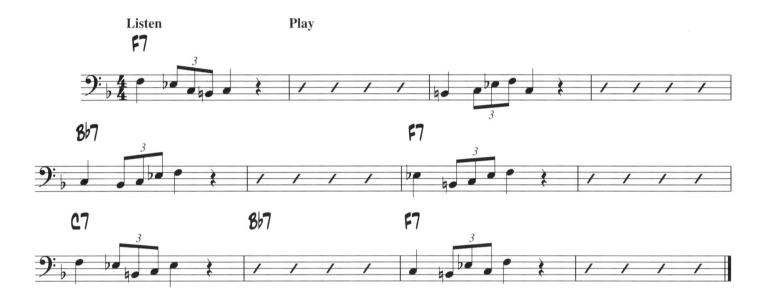

Use notes from groups 1 or 2 in this chorus, choosing the same group as you hear on the recording.

Write out a few of your own ideas. Use the F blues scale.

Create a 2-chorus solo using any techniques you have learned. Memorize your solo, and practice it along with the recording.

LESSON 8
READING

TROMBONE PART

This *chart* (written part) uses symbols and instructions that direct you to skip around the pages. When you get the hang of these symbols, you will see that they help reduce the number of written measures, and make the chart easier to read quickly, at a glance. Sometimes, these directions are called the chart's *road map*.

𝄐 Beats Drums   Pickup. Short introduction (less than a measure).

𝄋   Sign. Later, there will be a direction (D.S., or "from the sign") telling you to jump to this symbol from another location in the music.

⊕   Coda symbol. "Coda" is another word for "Ending." On the last chorus, skip from the first coda symbol to the second coda symbol (at the end of the piece). This symbol may also have the words "To Coda," or other directions (such as "last time only"). Often, you will just see the coda symbol by itself.

D.S. AL ⊕   From the sign (𝄋), and take the coda. Jump back to the sign (first measure, after the pickup), and play from there. When you reach the first coda symbol, skip ahead to the next coda symbol (at the end).

After Solos   When all solo choruses are finished, follow this direction.

B   Different choruses may be marked with different letters. In this tune, the head is marked "A," and the improvisation choruses are marked "B."

Solo   Solo chorus. Play this background part when other musicians in the band improvise. When you play this tune with your own band, you might repeat this section several times, depending on how many people solo. When you solo, then obviously, you won't play this written part.

Bass   Bass Part. Sometimes, you will see other instruments, especially when it is optional for the trombone to double them. A trombone can be a good substitute for a bass, if your band is looking for a different color.

Play "Do It Now" along with the recording and follow the written trombone part exactly. Even if you have it memorized already, follow the part as you play.

Do It Now

Trombone Part

By Matt Marvuglio

LEAD SHEET

Now play "Do It Now" with the recording, and work from the lead sheet.

LISTEN **14** PLAY

Do It Now
Trombone

By Matt Marvuglio

CHAPTER II
DAILY PRACTICE ROUTINE

WARM-UPS

Include this exercise in your five-part warm-up.

TECHNICAL

BLUES SCALE PRACTICE 1

Practice the blues scale in three keys. As before, practice each one five times, reading the music, and then five times from memory. Tomorrow, choose three other keys, and repeat the process every day until you can play the blues scale from memory in every key. Swing your eighths.

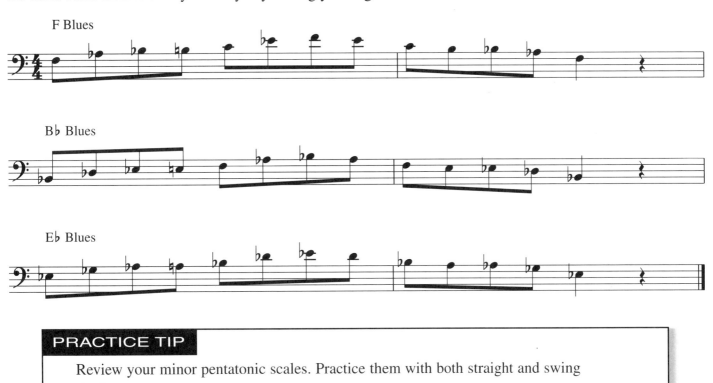

PRACTICE TIP

Review your minor pentatonic scales. Practice them with both straight and swing rhythms.

BLUES SCALE PRACTICE 2

Trombone Register: High Notes/Low Notes

Playing in different registers will give you new tone qualities and sounds. A phrase played in the low register has a certain energy and intensity. The same phrase played an octave higher will have a different feel and sound.

Practice this register exercise, and when you are ready, practice it along with the recording. Notice the different characters between the registers.

TROMBONE PLAYERS AND CHORDS

Guitar and keyboard players often play *chords*—three or more notes sounded simultaneously. Since the trombone can only sound one note at a time, it can only play the notes one after another, or as *arpeggios*. If your band has three or more trombones, then the section can play chords together.

"Do It Now" uses three different *dominant seventh* chords in its chord progression. Play them on your trombone.

Chord tones (the notes of a chord) are important resources for notes when you improvise, in the same way that scales are. Practice playing the chord tones for the chords in "Do It Now," using rhythms that fit the song's feel. Remember to swing your eighth notes. When you are ready, play this exercise along with the recording.

These exercises will help you develop your skills playing dominant seventh chords. It is in *descending form*— moving from high to low. Swing your eighth notes. Practice each chorus until you can play it easily, and then practice it with the recording.

The next exercise presents dominant seventh chords in *ascending form*—moving from low to high.

LISTEN 14 PLAY

TRANSPOSING PRACTICE

These exercises give you practice transposing licks to begin on all tones of a chord. When you are learning a new lick, practice it beginning on all tones of the tune's chords. This first exercise is an example of this technique. On your own, transpose the lick to begin on the tones of the **Bb7** and **C7** chords.

Transposing Exercise 1

You can also create lick transposition exercises that hook up with the recording.

Transposing Exercise 2

Transposing Exercise 3

LICKS

Here are some licks that you can practice and use in your solos. Practice transposing these licks to all the different chord tones, and create your own exercises based on them. Create and practice similar licks of your own.

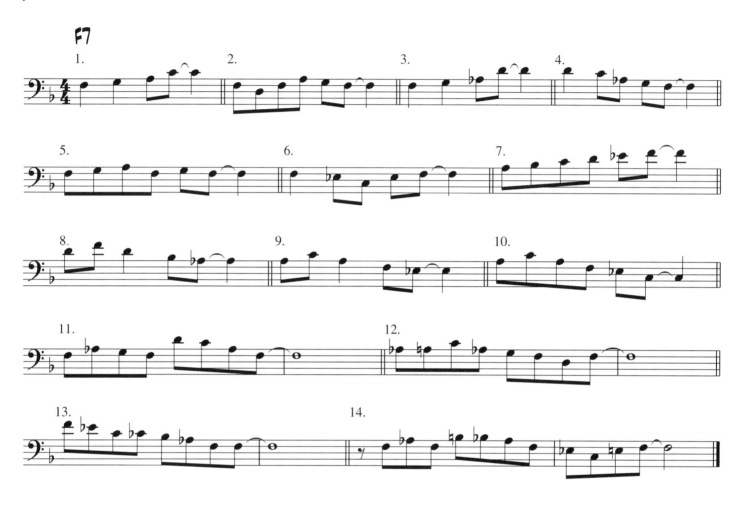

Practice going from the V chord (**C7**) to the IV chord (**B♭7**). Transposing licks works well at this part of a blues form.

BACKGROUNDS

Playing slightly different backgrounds during the melody and solo sections adds interest to the groove and gives the tune a sense of shape. The two background parts below vary in rhythm and articulation.

Practice these background lines with the recording. Play the first background part at the head, both at the beginning and at the end. Play the second one to support the soloist.

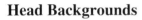

Head Backgrounds

Solo Backgrounds

CALL AND RESPONSE

1. Echo each lick, exactly as you hear it.
2. Improvise an answer to each lick. Use the same rhythm for each answer, but choose your own notes.

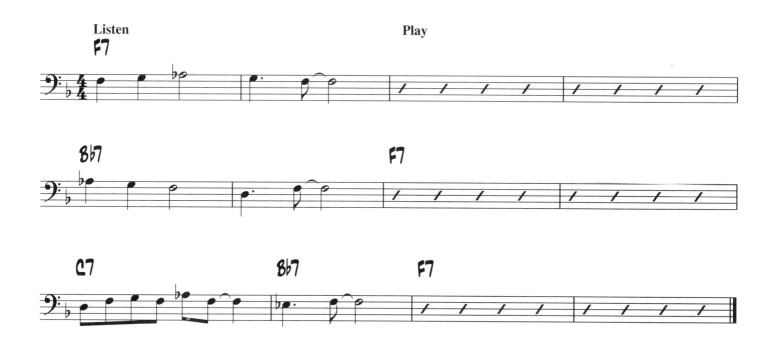

SOLO PRACTICE

Practice the first chorus of the solo to "Do It Now" along with the recording, reading the noteheads below. Use your ear to find the right rhythms.

When you can play this solo, play the full tune without looking at the music—first the melody, then the solo (play the above chorus twice), and then the melody again to end it. Follow your ear, and try to match the trombone on the recording.

PERFORMANCE TIP

If you make a mistake or get lost, keep your composure, and pretend that everything is going fine. Listen to the other instruments, hear what chords they are playing, and find your way back into the form. You can even practice getting lost and then finding your place. Start the recording at a random point within the track, and then follow your ear.

MEMORIZE

LISTEN **14** PLAY

Create your own solo using any techniques you have learned. Memorize your part, and then play through the tune with the recording as if you were performing it live. Keep your place in the form, and don't stop, whatever happens.

SUMMARY

FORM	ARRANGEMENT	HARMONY	SCALE
12-BAR BLUES	PICKUP: 2 BEATS DRUMS	F7 Bb7 C7	F BLUES
(1 CHORUS = 12 BARS)	2 CHORUS MELODY		
	2 CHORUS SOLO		
	1 CHORUS MELODY		
	END: 4 M.		

PLAY "DO IT NOW" WITH YOUR OWN BAND!

"I Just Wanna Be With You" is a *blues swing*. *Swing* is a dance-oriented, big-band style from the 1930s. To hear more swing, listen to Count Basie, Benny Goodman, the Squirrel Nut Zippers, Diana Krall, Branford Marsalis, Kevin Eubanks, Joanne Brackeen, Cherry Poppin' Daddies, Big Bad Voodoo Daddy, and trombonists Kid Ory, Jack Teagarden, J.C. Higginbotham, Vic Dickenson, and Tommy Dorsey.

LESSON 9
TECHNIQUE/THEORY

Listen to "I Just Wanna Be With You" and then play it along with the recording. This tune is a minor blues, similar to "Do It Now." The trombone is doubled by the sax and guitar. Look for similarities between the three phrases.

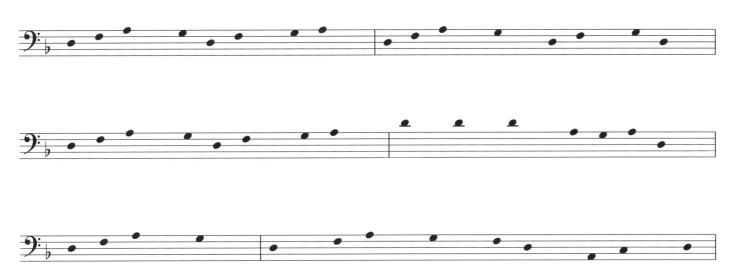

PICKUPS

Each phrase of "I Just Wanna Be With You" begins on a weak beat (an eighth note before beat 4), leading to a strong beat (beat 1). Notes leading to a strong beat are called *pickups*. While you are preparing to play, count beats along with the rhythm section. This will help you come in at the right time.

Feel the pulse, and count out loud. You come in after the third beat.

55

ARTICULATION: ACCENTS

Notes marked with accent (>) articulations are played louder than the rest so that they stand out. They are often the highest notes in the phrase.

Accents can make a phrase sound more spirited and energize a performance. Use them sparingly. If every note is accented, then nothing will stand out.

To accent a note, blow a sudden puff of air, as if you were fogging a window with warm air. Use a "tah" attack, like legato, but with a stronger T. Accented notes are held for their full value.

Practice accents along with the recording. Make accented notes stand out from the unaccented notes.

Accenting some of the notes in "I Just Wanna Be With You" will make the melody come alive—especially accenting notes that are unexpected, on beats that would ordinarily be weak, such as any eighth note off a beat, or beat 4. Practice it along with the recording. Make your accented notes stand out from the others.

PRACTICE TIP

Practice slowly. Before you can play something fast, you must be able to play it slowly.
Practice your positions, and try to hear the notes in your head before you play them.

LESSON 10
LEARNING THE GROOVE

LISTEN **17** PLAY

Listen to "I Just Wanna Be With You," and focus on the cymbals. This tune is a shuffle, like "Do It Now." There is a triplet feel under each beat. The main difference is that in this tune, the middle note in the triplet is left out. This is common in swing.

Shuffle
("Do It Now")

Swing Shuffle
("I Just Wanna...")

This syncopated "push-pull" feel is basic to jazz and r&b. Sometimes this feel is called a "double shuffle" because the drummer plays the same rhythm with both hands. In swing, the bass player usually plays a "walking" quarter-note bass line.

> ### PRACTICE TIP
>
> Record your practice. Use a small cassette or MiniDisc recorder, and record yourself playing along with the CD. Then listen to your recording. How accurately and consistently are you playing?

HOOKING UP TO SWING

Listen to "I Just Wanna Be With You." Find the beat, tap your foot, and clap along with the backbeat.

LISTEN **17** PLAY

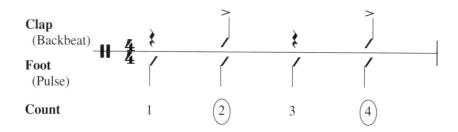

58

This tune has a swing feel, so count triplets on each beat as you play along with the backbeat. When you are ready, do this along with the recording. The circles show where to clap. The hi-hat matches your counting.

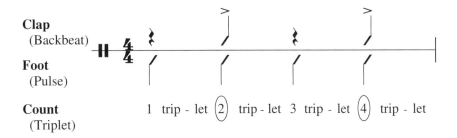

Clap swing eighth notes (see lesson 6).

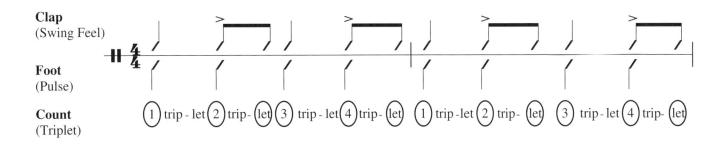

LEARNING "I JUST WANNA BE WITH YOU"

In this tune, the final note of the first measure is accented. Notes on the ordinarily weak beat 4 are usually not stressed, so this comes as a surprise—an interruption of the expected pulse. A rhythm such as this is called a *syncopation*. Syncopation is an important part of swing.

Clap the actual rhythms of the melody. When you are ready, clap along with the recording. Accent the notes that are marked.

LISTEN 17 PLAY

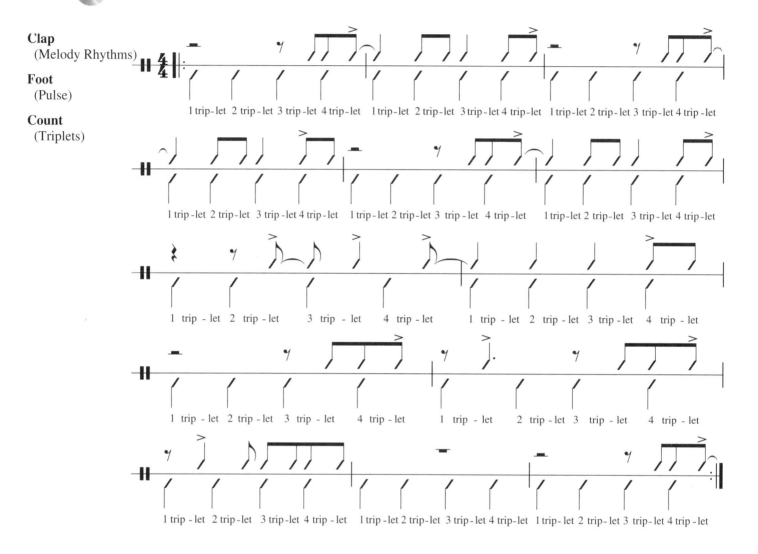

Play the actual part along with the recording. Tap your foot and count in your head, as you play. Use accents, and hook up with the groove.

LISTEN 17 PLAY

BACKGROUNDS

As discussed in chapter 2, background parts will often vary from when they support the head to when they support the solo. This gives the arrangement a sense of development and shape. In this tune, the rhythms of the background parts are the same as those played by the keyboard, so listen carefully and hook up with the keyboard when you play this part.

Practice this background to accompany the *head*.

Practice this background to accompany the *solo choruses*. Try taking it up an octave at the second solo chorus, and notice how this raises the energy level.

Create two of your own background parts—one for the head, the other for the solos. Write them out, and practice them with the recording.

LISTEN **17** PLAY

LESSON 11
IMPROVISATION

FORM AND ARRANGEMENT

Listen to "I Just Wanna Be With You," and follow the form. This tune is another 12-bar blues. The form of each chorus is twelve measures long and divided into three phrases, just like "Do It Now."

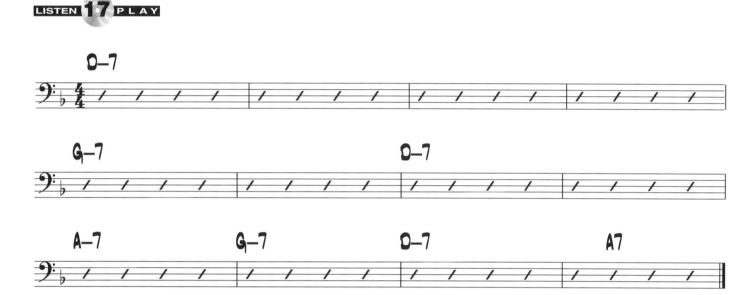

Listen to "I Just Wanna Be With You." Is there an introduction or ending? What part of the form did these added sections come from? Here is the arrangement used on the recording:

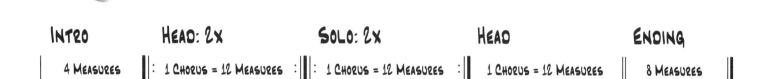

The intro and ending come from the form's last four measures. On the recording, the band chose to play the ending twice. This kind of repeated ending is called a *tag ending*.

PERFORMANCE TIP

Sometimes, a band may decide to "tag a tune" (play a tag ending) several times, building energy with each repetition. If things are going well and everyone is in the mood, a band may even make an ending longer than the rest of the tune. This is a place where people really let loose and have fun playing. When you listen to music, pay attention to what a band is doing at the end of a tune.

IDEAS FOR IMPROVISING

SCALES: D BLUES

The D blues scale is a good one for this tune. Play it on your trombone.

Practice the notes of the D blues scale over a wider range. Notice that it starts on a G. If you can, extend this range even farther, lower and higher.

D Blues Practice

LISTEN **18** PLAY

Practice the D blues scale through this wider melodic range, up and down, with the recording. Play each note in steady time, one per beat, and play as evenly as you can. Some notes, especially blue notes such as the A-flat, will jump out at you. Use these notes when you create your own solo.

CALL AND RESPONSE

1. Echo each phrase, exactly as you hear it.
2. Improvise an answer to each phrase. Imitate the sound and rhythmic feel of the phrase you hear, and use the notes from the D blues scale.

LISTEN **19** PLAY

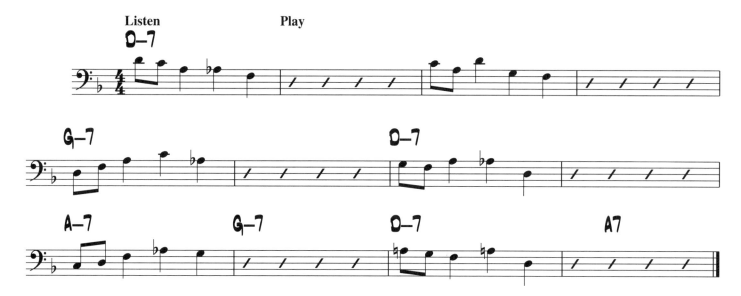

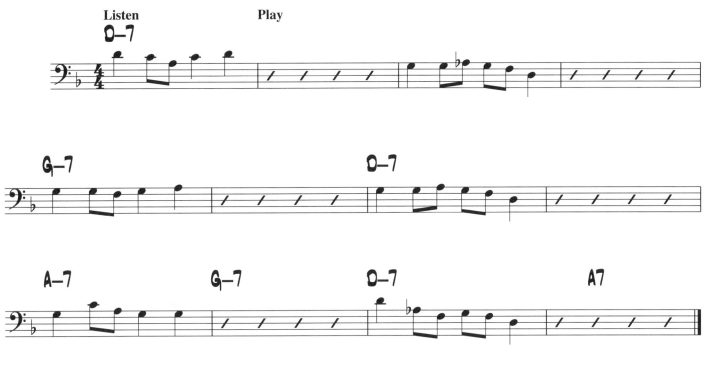

Write out a few of your own ideas. Use the D blues scale.

Create a 2-chorus solo using any techniques you have learned. Memorize your solo, and practice it along with the recording.

READING

TROMBONE PART

Play "I Just Wanna Be With You" while reading from the written trombone part. Practice playing the melody, the background parts, and your own improvised solo. Hook up with the recording.

I JUST WANNA BE WITH YOU

TROMBONE PART

BY MATT MARVUGLIO

LEAD SHEET

Play "I Just Wanna Be With You" from the lead sheet.

INTRO/ENDING Though this lead sheet doesn't show an introduction or ending, you and your band can create your own. The intro can be just drums, as you saw in "Do It Now," or it can come from the last line of the tune, as it does in the recording of this tune. Tag the ending at least three times, repeating the last four measures of the written part.

Since the melody is relatively short in length (twelve measures), you might want to play it twice when you are playing this tune with your own band. Play the pickups whenever you play the melody. You may or may not want to include them in your solo.

LISTEN **18** PLAY

I JUST WANNA BE WITH YOU
TROMBONE   BY MATT MARVUGLIO

CHAPTER III
DAILY PRACTICE ROUTINE

WARM-UPS

Include this exercise in your five-part warm-up.

Buzzing: Chromatics

Buzz each note without your horn until it sounds clear. Try it both with and without your mouthpiece.

Trombone Sound

Good control over your buzz will help improve your sound. Using different articulation "syllables," such as "dah," "tut,' and "hut," will also help you control your sound and make your notes sound unique. There are many other factors at work here also that will affect the sound you get out of your horn.

Here are some of the factors:
1. your diaphragm (the "support system");
2. how the air starts in your lungs;
3. the shape your throat and mouth make as the air passes through them;
4. how your mouthpiece sits on your lip.

To get a good sound, imagine that you are blowing warm air through your trombone, as if you were saying "haaaaaah." You can only do this if everything is relaxed, and your throat is open and relaxed. If anything is restricted, as if you were saying "heeuuh," less air will move, your breath will be colder, and your sound won't be as good.

Practice long tones on your trombone every day, and try to get as full and as warm a sound as you can. Here is an example of the kind of exercise you should do regularly. This one combines practicing long tones with practicing the D blues scale. Keep repeating this exercise for the whole track.

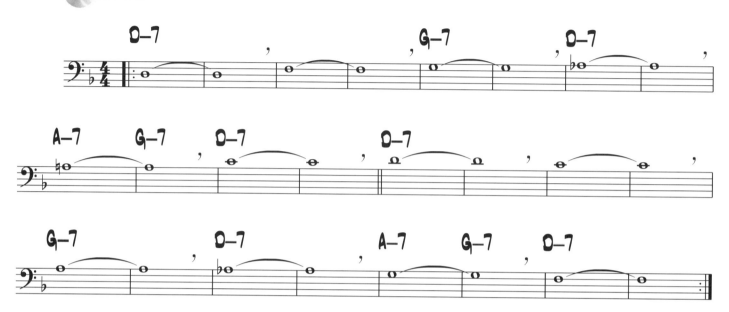

Start with lighter warm-ups that don't tax your lip too much, with a limited range and moderate volume. As you warm up, gradually increase the intensity of what you play. The following warm-ups use notes of the D minor pentatonic scale. Also play them based on the A and G minor pentatonic scales or blues scales based on D, A, and G.

Warm-up I

PRACTICE TIP

Try to relate your warm-ups to the music you will be playing. Since "I Just Wanna Be With You' uses the chords D–7, A–7, G–7, and A7, warm up using these chords or scales that relate to them. This tune has a swing feel, so swing your eighth notes in your warm-up exercises.

Warm-up 2

> **PRACTICE TIP**
>
> Practice using the entire range of your instrument. Try to play any of these warm-ups from any note of the scale. Add your own breath marks. Place them at the end of every two measures, after the first beat of every two measures, or any other place that feels comfortable and is musical.

TECHNIQUE

ARPEGGIO PRACTICE

ARTICULATIONS: STACCATO (SWING STYLE)

In swing, staccato is often marked with a (∧), which is slightly longer than a (.). To play staccato notes in swing, your tongue should move as if you were saying "tut."

Practice swing staccato articulation along with the recording. In this exercise, the staccato markings help emphasize the backbeat.

LISTEN **18** PLAY

LEGATO PRACTICE

The recorded version of "I Just Wanna Be With You" uses a combination of staccato and accented notes. Articulating these notes differently energizes the whole melody line. Try to make each articulation stand out. Practice the articulations as shown, and then play it along with the recording.

CHORDS

The lead sheet to "I Just Wanna Be With You" includes four different chords. The first three are *minor seventh chords* and the last one (A7) is a *dominant seventh* chord. The improvised solo makes good use of chord tones.

Practice chord tones with the recording. Notice how different the dominant seventh chord (A7 in the last measure) sounds—especially its note C♯. The different chord sound and the change in the groove make the last measure stand out and give the tune a unique character. It also helps the last measure to lead back to the first measure for when the form repeats. This is called a *turnaround* because it "turns the form around" back to the beginning.

IMPROVISATION PRACTICE

Though warm-up licks often begin on the chord root, when you are creating your own licks for solos or backgrounds, try to begin on other pitches. It will make your solo more interesting.

In this exercise, start each measure on the pitch given. Using the written rhythms, fill in your own pitches to finish each measure. Find three or four different ways of completing each phrase. Then try it using your own rhythms.

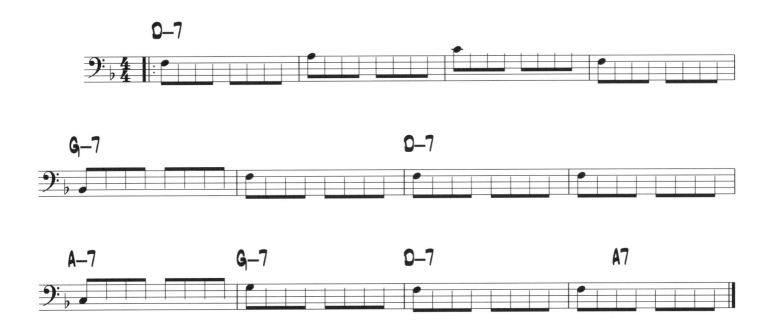

PRACTICE TIP
Sing your part before you play it. This will help you on the call and response exercises, and whenever you learn music generally.

CALL AND RESPONSE

1. Echo each phrase, exactly as you hear it.
2. Improvise an answer to each phrase. Imitate the sound and rhythmic feel of the phrase you hear, and use the notes from the D blues scale.

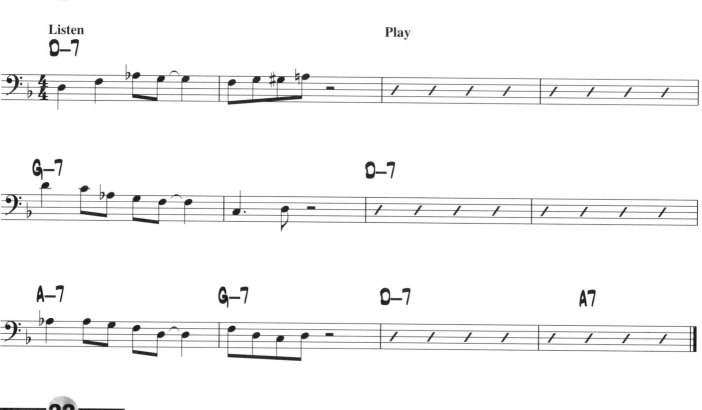

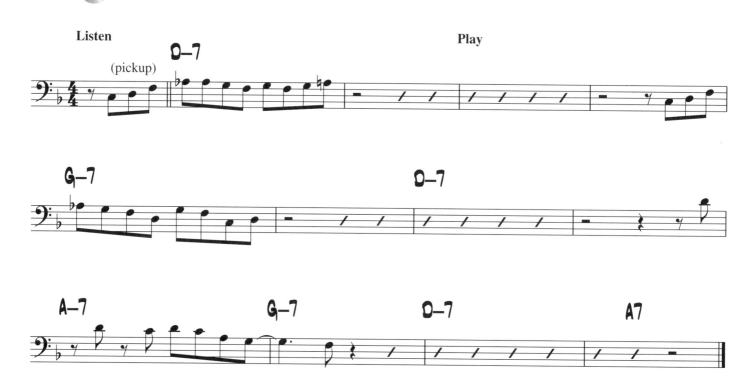

IMPROVING USING CHORD TONES

LISTEN **18** PLAY

Practice this trombone solo, and then play it along with the recording. Notice the use of chord tones.

Create some of your own chord-tone licks.

LISTEN **18** PLAY

Create a 2-chorus solo using any techniques you have learned. Memorize your solo, and practice it along with the recording.

SOLO PRACTICE

Practice the recorded trombone solo to "I Just Wanna Be With You." When you are ready, play along with the recording.

MEMORIZE

Work on playing your own, personal interpretation of the melody of "I Just Wanna Be With You," with your own articulations and phrasing. Record yourself playing it along with the CD. Next, work on playing your own solos based on its chord progression, song form, and groove. Record your solos. Write down your favorite one and memorize it.

SUMMARY

FORM	ARRANGEMENT	HARMONY	SCALE
12-BAR BLUES (1 CHORUS = 12 BARS)	INTRO: 4 M. 2 CHORUS MELODY 2 CHORUS SOLO 1 CHORUS MELODY END: 8 M.	D-7 G-7 A-7 A7	D BLUES

PLAY "I JUST WANNA BE WITH YOU" WITH YOUR OWN BAND!

"Leave Me Alone" is a *funk* tune. Funk has its roots in New Orleans street music. It started in the late 1960s, and is a combination of rock, r&b, Motown, jazz, and blues. Funk has also influenced many rap artists. To hear more funk, listen to James Brown, Tower of Power, Kool and the Gang, the Meters, the Yellowjackets, Chaka Khan, Tina Turner, the Red Hot Chili Peppers, and trombonist Fred Wesley.

LESSON 13
TECHNIQUE/THEORY

Listen to "Leave Me Alone," and play along with the recording. Try to match the trombone playing the melody.

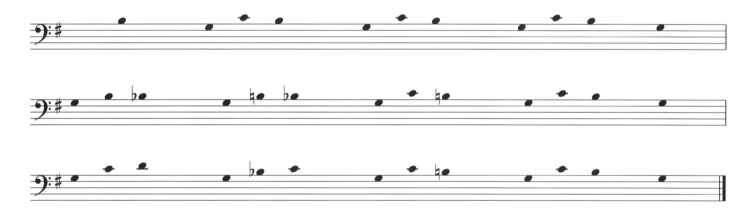

ARTICULATION: LEGATO

Notes marked with legato (–) articulations in jazz and pop styles are played for their full rhythmic value. Legato marks are similar to slurs, but the articulations are marked on individual notes, rather than whole phrases. When you are *sustaining* (holding) a legato note, counting eighth notes as you play will help you to

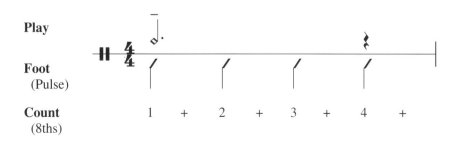

Practice playing notes legato along with the recording. Count eighth-note subdivisions in your head, and start and stop your notes as precisely as you can.

Long, legato notes in a melody let listeners hear the rhythm section playing the groove. Short, staccato notes help the melody sound more like a part of the rhythm section. You can use a combination of both kinds of articulation.

Practice this articulation exercise with the recording.

LONG PHRASES AND BREATHING

Try to play each 4-measure phrase of "Leave Me Alone" in a single breath. This will give each phrase a feeling of continuity. You will need to take a deep breath before you begin each phrase.

When you are looking at a new piece of music and trying to determine where to breathe, the first place to try is during rests. If you need to breathe before you see a rest, look for any natural place in the phrase, in which the phrase or the sense of forward motion won't sound interrupted. You can mark these places with optional breath marks (ʾ). Only breathe there if you have to.

Practice the melody to "Leave Me Alone" with the recording, and try to breathe only at the end of each 4-bar phrase. If you need to breathe earlier, do so only at the optional breath marks.

LESSON 14
LEARNING THE GROOVE

HOOKING UP TO FUNK

LISTEN **23** PLAY

Listen to "Leave Me Alone." This funk groove has its roots in New Orleans street music—funky march music played on marching instruments (snare drums, bass drums, and so on) still found in the Mardi Gras parades each spring. Many New Orleans artists were important to the development of funk.

Funk rhythms are played with less of a swing feel than blues. There is an underlying sixteenth-note feel, similar to rock, so count "1 e + a, 2 e + a, 3 e + a, 4 e + a," as you play. In funk, the backbeat is especially accented, usually by the snare drum.

This exercise will help you hook up to funk. Play along with the recording and match the trombone. The music is written out below. Find the beat, and play the melody. It emphasizes the strong, funk backbeat.

LISTEN **25** PLAY

SYNCOPATIONS AND ARTICULATIONS

How you articulate syncopations changes how they feel in the groove. In this next example, each lick is played legato and then staccato. Give each one a unique sound. Echo each lick exactly as you hear it, focusing on articulations. You may find that they are easier to hear than to read, so listen carefully, and try to copy what you hear.

LISTEN **26** PLAY

BACKGROUNDS

Practice these background parts along with the recording. Listen carefully to the other instruments, and be sure to play the sixteenth notes exactly in time, without rushing. Watch the articulations!

When you perform this tune, only play the first background part on the second time through the head.

LISTEN **23** PLAY

2nd time only

Play this background part behind the solos.

Solo Backgrounds

LESSON 15
IMPROVISATION

FORM AND ARRANGEMENT

Listen to "Leave Me Alone," and follow the form. This funk tune follows the 12-bar blues form.

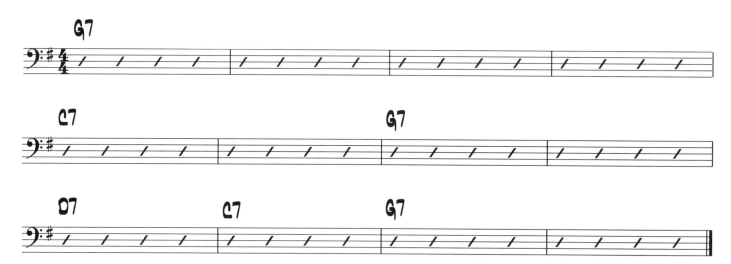

On the recording, the arrangement begins with a 4-measure introduction, featuring the rhythm section playing the groove.

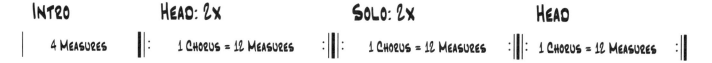

IDEAS FOR IMPROVISING

SCALES: G BLUES

The G blues scale is a good choice for use with this tune. Play it on your trombone.

Practice the notes of the G blues scale over a wider range.

CHORDS

The chords to "Leave Me Alone" are all the same type: dominant seven chords, discussed in chapter 2. These chords have the same sound, with the same *intervals*—the distances between pitches. The only change is that they are *transposed*; they begin on different notes. When you improvise, favor the chord tones of the symbol shown above the staff. This is called "making the changes,"or interpreting the song's chords in your own way.

Practice the chord tones to "Leave Me Alone." Below each tone is an interval number showing the note's relationship to the chord root. Since all chords in this tune are dominant-7 chords, the interval numbers are the same: root, 3, 5, ♭7.

RIFFS

Another good improvisation technique is to create a lick and then repeat it over and over. This repetition of a lick is called a *riff*. The lick's notes may come from a scale, from chord tones, from melody notes, or a combination of all three.

In the next exercise, we will play a riff built on this lick. Practice it until you can play it easily.

Echo each riff exactly as you hear it.

LISTEN **27** PLAY

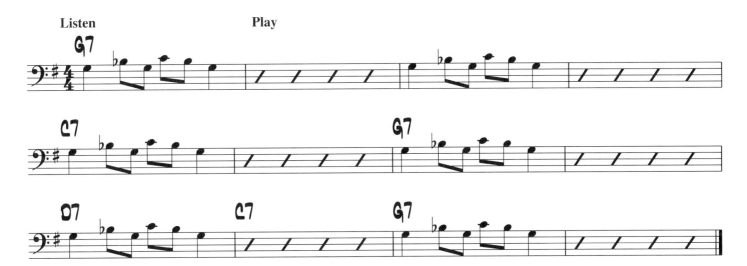

WRITE YOUR OWN SINGLE RIFF SOLO

Create your own riff-based solo to "Leave Me Alone." Make sure the riff you create sounds good over all the chords. Write it out, and practice it along with the recording.

LISTEN **24** PLAY

TRANSPOSING LICKS

To make a single lick sound good over several different chords, you have to keep it simple and only use a couple of pitches. If you want to use a more complex riff, you can transpose the lick to different notes, similar to how the dominant-7 chords earlier were transposed to begin on different roots.

Practice this lick a few times until you can play it easily. Since it is based on the tune's first chord (G7), you can think of it as being in the "original" key. Interval numbers are shown below each note.

To transpose this lick, move its root to the root of each new chord (**C7** and **D7**), and then use the same intervals to find the other notes. Practice the lick based on all three chords until you can play them easily.

Echo each riff exactly as you hear it.

LISTEN **28** PLAY

WRITE YOUR OWN TRANSPOSING RIFF SOLO

Create your own riff-based solo to "Leave Me Alone." Transpose the same riff over all the chords. Write it out, and practice it along with the recording.

LISTEN **24** PLAY

TROMBONE PART

Play "Leave Me Alone" along with the recording, using the written trombone part.

CUE NOTES   The small notes in measures 1 to 4 are *cue notes* showing the bass guitar part. Read along with the bass, and use the cue notes to help you come in on time.

LISTEN **24** PLAY

LEAVE ME ALONE

TROMBONE PART

BY MATT MARVUGLIO

LEAD SHEET

Play "Leave Me Alone," and follow along with the lead sheet. Create your own riff-based solo. Try transposing the licks by ear.

LISTEN 24 PLAY

Leave Me Alone

Trombone

By Matt Marvuglio

PRACTICE TIP

Memorizing your notes makes it easier to follow arrangement directions, such as "D.S. al ⊕."

CHAPTER IV
DAILY PRACTICE ROUTINE

WARM-UPS

Include this exercise in your five-part warm-up.

Slurs: 4-Note Slow Slurs

Add this after you do your 2-and 3-note slurs (see chapters 1 and 2). Practice all three slurring exercises at the same tempo. Slow the other two down, if you need to.

Use these exercises as part of your warm-up routine for this tune. Add your own breath marks.

C7

> **PRACTICE TIP**
>
> Create your own warm-up exercise based on the **D7** chord. Use the exercises for **G7** and
> **C7** as your models.

LICK PRACTICE

Practice these licks. When you create a solo for this tune, any licks from this first set can be used over the **G7** measures.

G7

These licks will work well on measures 9 and 10. They all make use of the transposition techniques discussed in the lessons.

FUNK RHYTHMS

Practice this solo with the recording. Choose a combination of articulations to make your part groove with the rhythm section. Write your articulations into the score below.

LISTEN **24** PLAY

MAKING THE CHANGES

This solo draws its notes from three different sources. During **G7** measures, the notes come from the G blues scale. During the **C7** measures, the notes come from the chord tones of **C7**. During the **D7** measure, the notes come from chord tones of **D7**. Practice it alone first, and when you're ready, play it with the recording.

LISTEN **24** PLAY

SOLO PRACTICE

Practice the recorded solo to "Leave Me Alone." Notice that it is an embellished form of the melody. Before you play, read along with the recording, and position the notes on the trombone without blowing—just move the slide. When you are ready, play along with the recording.

MEMORIZE

LISTEN **24** P L A Y

Create your own solo using any of the techniques you have learned, and write it out. Practice it, memorize it, and then record yourself playing the whole tune along with the recording.

SUMMARY

FORM
12-BAR BLUES
(1 CHORUS = 12 BARS)

ARRANGEMENT
INTRO: 4 M.
2 CHORUS MELODY
2 CHORUS SOLO
1 CHORUS MELODY

HARMONY
G7   C7   D7

SCALE
G BLUES

PLAY "LEAVE ME ALONE" WITH YOUR OWN BAND!

<table>
<tr><td>**PLAYING LIGHT FUNK**</td><td>**CHAPTER V**</td></tr>
</table>

"Affordable" is another funk tune, but it is lighter, with more of a feeling of open space. This style is popular with smooth-jazz artists. To hear more light funk, listen to artists such as David Sanborn, Earl Klugh, Walter Beasley, the Rippingtons, Dave Grusin, Kenny G, Bob James, and Anita Baker.

LESSON 17
TECHNIQUE/THEORY

Listen to "Affordable," and then play along with the recording. Try to match the recorded melody.

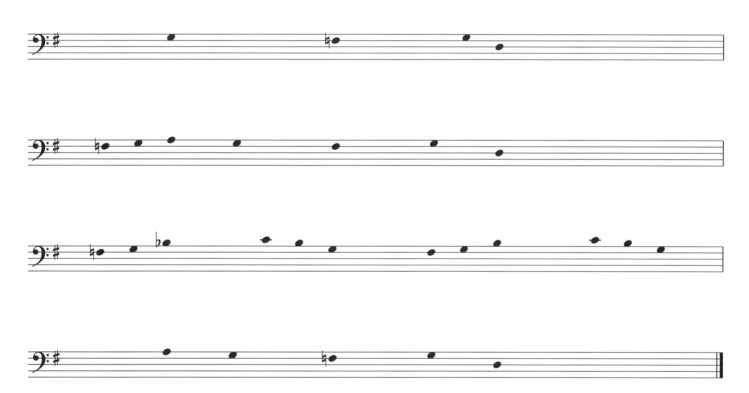

DYNAMICS

The melody of "Affordable" is made mostly of long, drawn-out notes. The trombone player on the recording makes this melody more interesting by changing the notes' *dynamics*—their loudness and softness. In this tune, the last notes of each phrase generally *decrescendo* (gradually become softer). The notation for decrescendos is a wedge (sometimes called a *hairpin*) opening to the left ($>$). This shows where the sound should be louder (above the lines' widest point) and where it should be softer (above where the lines meet). The opposite of a decrescendo is a *crescendo* (gradually growing louder), which opens to the right ($<$).

Practice the melody to "Affordable" with the recording, and decrescendo at the end of phrases 1, 2, and 4. Notice how dynamics help to shape the melody.

LISTEN **29** PLAY

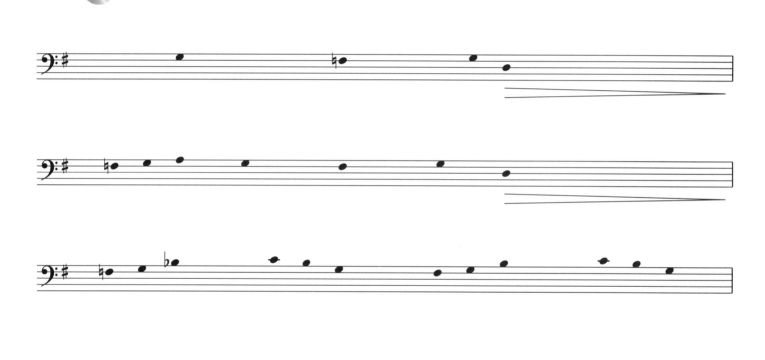

LESSON 18
LEARNING THE GROOVE

HOOKING UP TO LIGHT FUNK

LISTEN 29 PLAY

Listen to "Affordable." This groove is built around eighth notes, with some syncopated sixteenths in the B section. Notice that the bass guitar hooks up with the bass drum.

To learn this feel, practice counting sixteenths, leaving out the middle two sixteenths of each beat. Count out loud, along with a metronome or click track on the quarter-note pulse.

1   e   +   a   2   (e) (+) a   3 think think a   4   a   1   a 2   a 3   a 4   a

"Affordable" is a *light* funk tune. Like all funk music, eighth notes are played straight, not with a swing feel. The rhythm section plays fewer notes than they do in other styles of music. This makes the melody stand out even more than it does on the other tunes. What other elements of funk do you notice?

Listen to "Affordable." Find the pulse, and feel the sixteenth-note subdivisions. Notice that the backbeat is still emphasized, but it is lighter than it was in heavy funk.

TROMBONE IN THE RHYTHM SECTION

To hook up to a groove, try playing the rhythm section's parts along with the recording. This trombone line combines the bass, guitar, and keyboard parts. Feel the backbeat and the sixteenth notes as you play.

There are two different grooves in this tune. Play this first riff during phrases 1, 2, and 4, and at the introduction.

LISTEN 30 PLAY

Play this riff during phrase 3.

LISTEN 31 PLAY

BACKGROUNDS

When you play backgrounds, think of yourself as part of the rhythm section. Hook up with the drums, bass, guitar, and keyboard. Notice how your background part hooks up with the keyboard part.

LISTEN 29 PLAY

LESSON 19
IMPROVISATION

FORM AND ARRANGEMENT

Listen to "Affordable," and follow the 16-bar form.

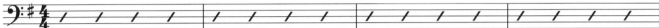

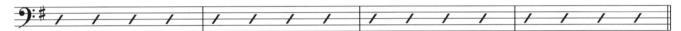

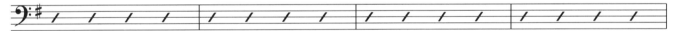

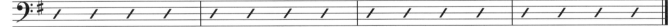

From practicing the keyboard, guitar, and bass parts, you can tell that there are two primary musical ideas in this tune. When you play the melody you can hear that there are two contrasting sections. Idea A is very sparse. It lasts for eight measures, with two phrases of trombone melody. Idea B is in a more regular rhythm. It lasts for four measures. Then idea A returns for four measures. This form can be described as "AABA."

> **PRACTICE TIP**
>
> The 4-measure return of idea A at the end of the form may be confused with the eight measures of idea A that begin the new chorus. Altogether, there are twelve measures of this idea, so keep careful count.

Listen to the whole tune. Sing the melody while the trombone plays the solo, and keep your place in the form. What is the arrangement on the recording? Is there an introduction or ending? Check your answer against the summary at the end of this chapter.

IDEAS FOR IMPROVISING

SCALES: G MAJOR AND MINOR PENTATONIC

The G major pentatonic scale will work well for improvising on this tune's A sections.

The G minor pentatonic scale will work well for improvising on this tune's B section.

CALL AND RESPONSE

1. Echo each phrase, exactly as you hear it.
2. Improvise an answer to each phrase. Imitate the sound and rhythmic feel of the phase you hear, and use the notes from the G pentatonic scales.

EMBELLISHING THE MELODY

The song melody is an excellent source of ideas for notes and licks. Whenever you play the melody, you contribute to the musical mood. The melody identifies the spirit and character of the song.

Think of the song melody as a compass. As you improvise, use it as your guide. Keep the melody at your solo's center, and improvise by adding or removing a few notes, or by varying their rhythm. Such changes are called *embellishments*.

Practice this embellished version of "Affordable." When you're ready, practice it along with the recording.

Try playing the embellished version above "against" the original song melody. You can feel the added notes when you play them along with the original melody track.

Write out your own embellished version of the melody. Use the G pentatonic scales and the melody itself as sources for notes.

Create a 1-chorus solo using any techniques you have learned. Memorize your solo, and practice it along with the recording.

LESSON 20
READING

TROMBONE PART

TROMBONE Part label. The written parts you have been using were written specifically for trombones. Trombones are *non-transposing* (also called "concert") instruments, meaning that the note names on a trombone are the actual pitches. Trombone parts are usually written in bass clef. Trumpets, saxophones, and some other instruments read *transposed* music. This will be in another key. If a transposing instrument reads your trombone part, the notes will sound in the wrong key, unless the musician can transpose at sight. Their parts might also be in a different clef.

This is done because the strongest registers of other instruments don't always fit on a regular staff. If the notes were written where they sound, they might have to read a lot more ledger lines. Transposing their part reduces the number of ledger lines and makes reading easier for them. But it also means that everyone must be sure that they are reading the correct part.

Play "Affordable" while reading the trombone part, and solo where indicated. Use the cue notes to help you keep your place.

LISTEN **33** PLAY

AFFORDABLE
TROMBONE PART
BY MATT MARVUGLIO

Play "Affordable" while reading the lead sheet.

CHAPTER V
DAILY PRACTICE ROUTINE

WARM-UPS

Long Tones: Descending Long Tones

Include this exercise in your five-part warm-up. Start each long-tone group with a "tu" syllable. Rest after each position. Practice this exercise as slowly as you can.

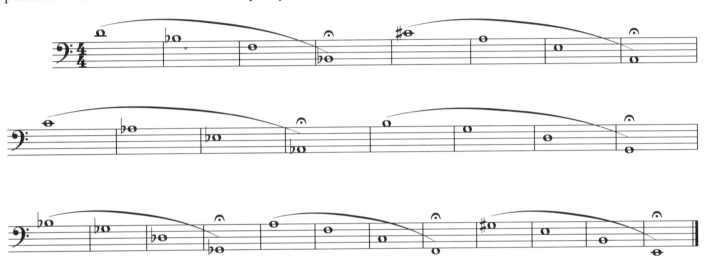

VIBRATO

Vibrato is a slight, controlled vibration of a note's pitch, giving it a singing quality. In the older styles, such as early jazz, vibrato was typically wide and rapid. In more contemporary trombone playing styles, vibrato is generally used more sparingly.

In contemporary pop, r&b, rock, and jazz trombone playing styles, the speed and depth (variation of pitch) of vibrato are more varied. Many times, long notes begin straight, and then vibrato is added gradually. By listening to a lot of music, you will develop your own sense for when to use vibrato.

There are two ways of adding vibrato to a note. To use *lip vibrato,* move your jaw up and down, as if you were saying "ya-ya." To use *slide vibrato*, move your slide quickly on each side of the pitch, about an inch. Keep the main pitch at the center of the vibrato.

There are many ways that great trombonists have used vibrato. Some players used slide vibrato: Tommy Dorsey, Urbie Green, Wayne Andre, Bill Watrous. Some players used lip vibrato: Bill Harris, Roswell Rudd, Gary Valente. Some players used little or no vibrato: J.J. Johnson, Curtis Fuller, Slide Hampton.

Practice long tones along with the recording. Start each note straight, then gradually add more and more vibrato to it, following the curvy line. This is called *terminal vibrato* because each note starts straight and then ends (terminates) with vibrato.

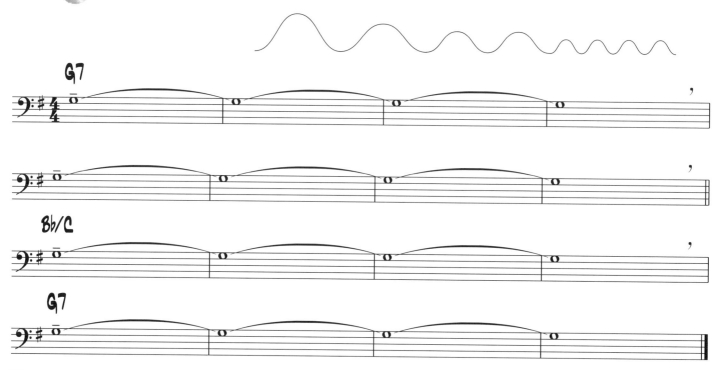

DYNAMICS AND VIBRATO

Try combining vibrato with dynamics, adding just a touch of vibrato at the end of phrases 1, 2, and 4. Don't overdo it! Just a little vibrato will sound great.

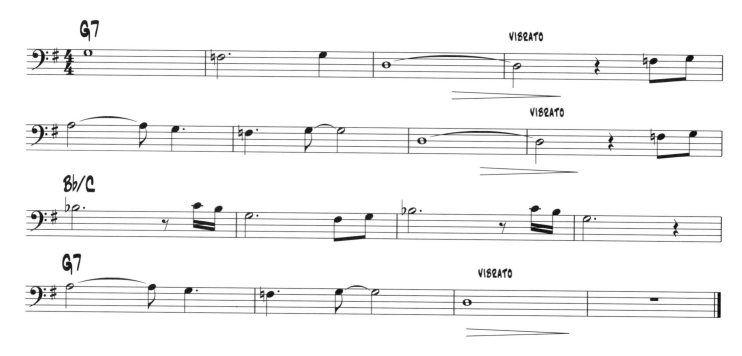

PENTATONIC SCALE PRACTICE

Create a solo using the tune's chords and notes of the G pentatonic scales, shown below the trombone staff. Try using different rhythms that hook up to the light funk groove. Practice your solo with the recording.

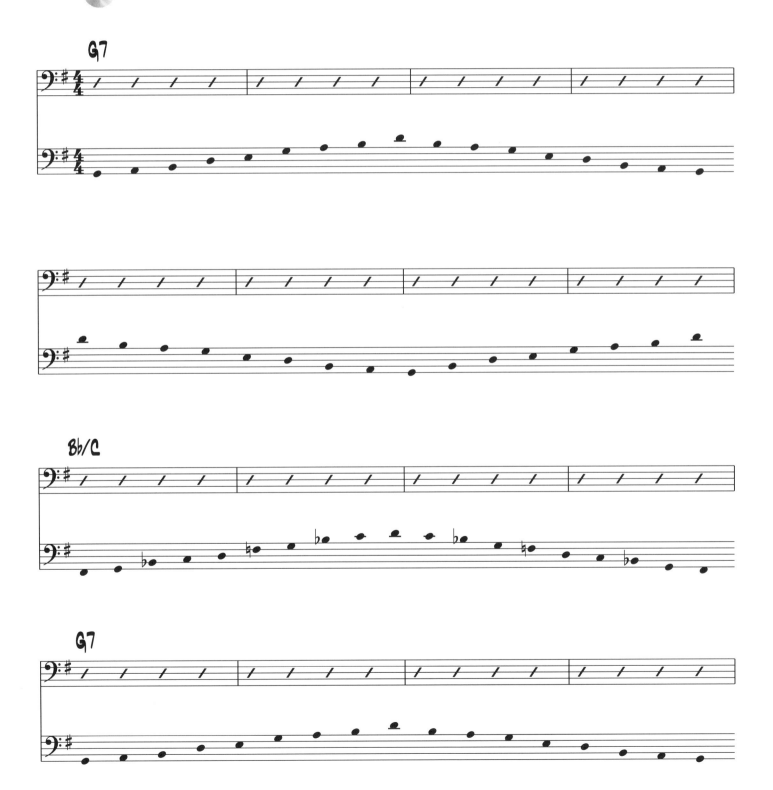

MEMORIZE

Create your own solo using any of the techniques you have learned, and write it out. Practice it, memorize it, and then record yourself playing the whole tune along with the CD.

SUMMARY

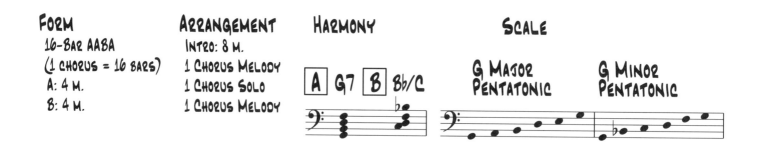

FORM	ARRANGEMENT	HARMONY	SCALE	
16-BAR AABA	INTRO: 8 M.			
(1 CHORUS = 16 BARS)	1 CHORUS MELODY	A G7 B Bb/C	G MAJOR PENTATONIC	G MINOR PENTATONIC
A: 4 M.	1 CHORUS SOLO			
B: 4 M.	1 CHORUS MELODY			

PLAY "AFFORDABLE" WITH YOUR OWN BAND!

"Don't Look Down" is a *hard rock* tune. Hard rock first appeared in the late 1960s. It has characteristic heavy bass, long, drawn-out chords, and amplified instruments. To hear more hard rock, listen to artists such as Aerosmith, Metallica, Powerman 5000, the Allman Brothers Band, Rob Zombie, Godsmack, 311, Stone Temple Pilots, Black Crowes, Steve Vai, and Smashing Pumpkins.

LESSON 21
TECHNIQUE/THEORY

Listen to "Don't Look Down," and then play the melody along with the recording. The trombone is doubled by the sax and guitar. This tune has two different parts.

The first part has these four phrases.

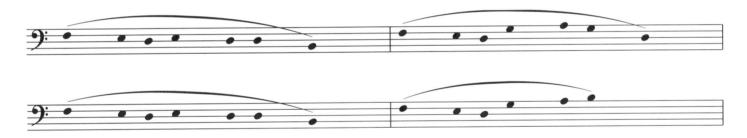

The second part has a riff that repeats four times.

It ends with the bass riff, played twice.

HIGH REGISTER

The high register can lend a great deal of energy and intensity to music, especially when it is played loudly. For hard rock, you may want to transpose part or all of the melody up an octave, and use some high notes in your solo.

Practice "Don't Look Down" with some of the phrases transposed to the higher octave, and notice their increased intensity. Focus on playing in tune.

LISTEN 34 PLAY

PRACTICE TIP

Develop the ability to transpose up or down an octave by sight. Lead sheets are often written in the middle register so that they can be read by many different instruments, but that may not be the best register for where you should play it.

LESSON 22
LEARNING THE GROOVE

HOOKING UP TO ROCK

Listen to "Don't Look Down." This tune has a standard rock/metal groove. It is a heavy feel, with very simple drum and bass parts. These parts must be simple because they are intended to be played in large arenas, where echoes would make busier parts sound muddy. It's a case of "less is more."

During the solos, the guitar doubles the bass, playing power chords in the second part. The keyboard plays sustained chords with an organ sound.

LISTEN 35 PLAY

Listen to the first part of "Don't Look Down." Tap your foot along with the quarter-note pulse, and clap along with the backbeat.

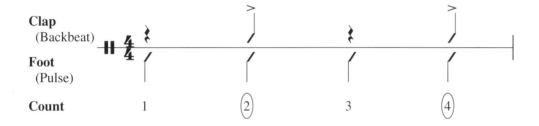

Try the same thing again. This time count the sixteenth notes out loud: 1e+a, 2e+a, 3e+a, 4e+a.

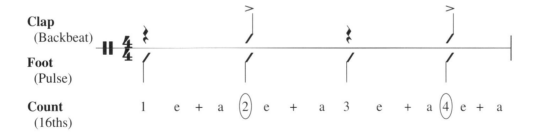

LEARNING "DON'T LOOK DOWN"

In the first part of this tune, the bass guitar plays a syncopated sixteenth-note riff. You hook up with that riff while you play the melody, and then you actually play the riff at the ending.

First, practice clapping the rhythms.

LISTEN **35** PLAY

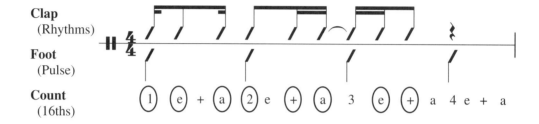

Next, play the actual notes. Hook up with the rhythm section. If you like, you can play this riff instead of the melody along with the A section of the full-band track.

LISTEN **35** PLAY

The second part of this tune also has a syncopated sixteenth-note figure. Practice clapping the rhythms to this lick (also used at the Intro).

LISTEN **36** PLAY

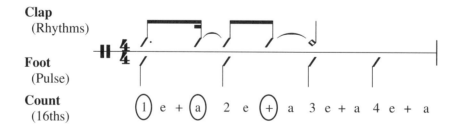

Practice the notes.

LISTEN **36** PLAY

Practice the whole tune along with the recording, and hook up with the rhythm section.

LISTEN **34** PLAY

BACKGROUNDS

Practice these background lines along with the recording. Then create similar background lines of your own.

LISTEN **34** PLAY

LESSON 23
IMPROVISATION

FORM AND ARRANGEMENT

LISTEN **34** PLAY

Listen to the recording, and try to figure out the form and arrangement by ear. How long does each section of the form last? Is there an introduction or ending? For how many measures or beats does each chord last? Write down as much information as you can. Check your answers against the summary at the end of this chapter.

This tune has a 20-bar AB form. Part A has an active riff that builds a lot of tension. It lasts for sixteen measures. Part B is less active than the first part. It lasts for four measures. There is a 4-measure introduction at the beginning of the tune. It comes from the B section.

IDEAS FOR IMPROVISING

SCALES: G MAJOR AND MINOR PENTATONIC

The G major pentatonic scale will work well for improvising on this tune's A section.

The G minor pentatonic scale will work well for improvising on this tune's B section.

Practice both these scales. You can use both of them when you improvise, depending upon the chord.

114

CALL AND RESPONSE

Mixing Chord Tones and Pentatonic Scales

1. Echo the rhythm of each phrase exactly.
2. Improvise an answer to each phrase. Copy the rhythms of the recorded licks but choose your own notes, based on the source indicated above the staff.

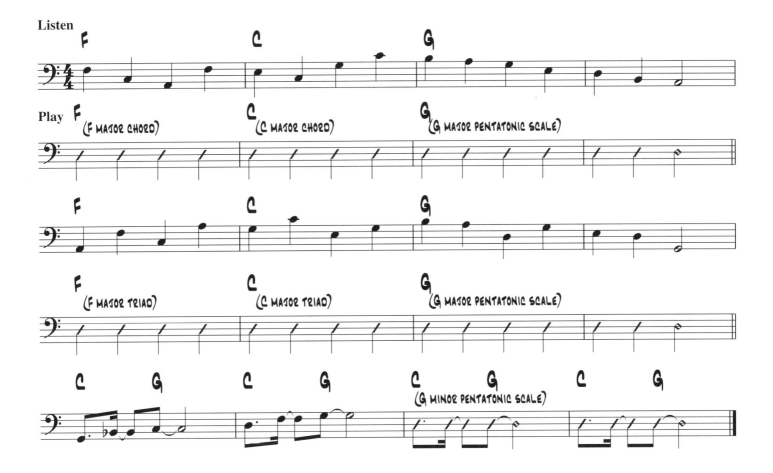

Write out a few of your own ideas.

Create a 1-chorus solo using any techniques you have learned. Memorize your solo, and practice it along with the recording.

LESSON 24
READING

TROMBONE PART

Play "Don't Look Down" along with the recording. Use the written trombone part. If you can, try the melody up an octave.

 First and second ending markings. The first time you play these measures, play the *first ending*—the measures under the number 1. Then return to the begin-repeat sign (‖:). The second time you play these measures, skip the first ending and play the *second ending*—the measures under the number 2. Then, continue through the rest of the form.

DON'T LOOK DOWN
TROMBONE PART

BY MATT MARVUGLIO

LISTEN 38 PLAY

PERFORMANCE TIP

When you practice from a lead sheet, use it to help you keep your place. Even when you solo, follow the music as you play. This will help you to keep track of the form, so you can memorize it.

LEAD SHEET

Play your own part to "Don't Look Down," and follow along with the lead sheet.

LISTEN 38 PLAY

DON'T LOOK DOWN

TROMBONE

"HARD ROCK" ♩ = 88

BY MATT MARVUGLIO

CHAPTER VI
DAILY PRACTICE ROUTINE

EMBELLISHMENT PRACTICE

Practice embellishing the melody to "Don't Look Down." Play the written 4-bar embellished melody and then your own 4-bar embellished melody. Include the original melody notes, on their original beats, in your embellished melody.

SOLO PRACTICE

Practice the recorded solo along with the CD.

LISTEN **34** PLAY

MEMORIZE

LISTEN 38 PLAY

Create your own solo using any of the techniques you have learned, and write it out. Practice it, memorize it, and then record yourself playing the whole tune along with the recording.

SUMMARY

FORM	ARRANGEMENT	HARMONY	SCALE
20-BAR AB FORM	INTRO: 4 M.		
(1 CHORUS = 20 BARS)	1 CHORUS MELODY		G MAJOR PENTATONIC G MINOR PENTATONIC
A: 16 M.	1 CHORUS SOLO	F C G	
B: 4 M.	1 CHORUS MELODY		
	END: 2 M.		

PLAY "DON'T LOOK DOWN" WITH YOUR OWN BAND!

PLAYING BOSSA NOVA

CHAPTER VII

"Take Your Time" is a *bossa nova* tune. Bossa nova began in Brazil, combining American jazz and an Afro-Brazilian form of dance music called *samba*. To hear more bossa nova, listen to Stan Getz, Antonio Carlos Jobim, Eliane Elias, Astrud Gilberto, Flora Purim, Dave Valentine, Spyro Gyra, and trombonists Barry Rogers and Papo Vasquez.

LESSON 25
TECHNIQUE/THEORY

LISTEN **39** PLAY

Listen to "Take Your Time" on the recording. The melody is in two long phrases. Practice it along with the recording, and try to match the melody.

This is the first phrase.

This is the second phrase.

PRACTICE TIP

Take a deep breath before you play each of the above phrases. If you begin each phrase with enough air, you'll be able to play those low notes with a clear, full tone.

LOW REGISTER

Practicing low notes will help you develop a full sound in the middle and high registers as well. These notes require more air to be blown through the horn. Opening your jaw to create a bigger oral cavity will help your notes to sound big and round. Think more "taw" (as in "tawny"), as opposed to "tah" (as in "top").

Practice this low-register exercise along with the recording. Maintain a big, full sound.

LESSON 26
LEARNING THE GROOVE

HOOKING UP TO BOSSA NOVA

Listen to "Take Your Time." This tune is a bossa nova, a style of music that originated in Brazil. Throughout the tune, a 2-bar rhythmic pattern repeats. This repeating pattern is an essential part of bossa nova. The drum plays it on a rim click.

Repeating rhythmic structures are at the heart of much African-based music, including Afro-Caribbean and most South and Latin American styles.

> **PRACTICE TIP**
>
> A good way to practice hooking up with a tune is to play all the other instruments' parts.

Listen to the drums on the recording, and follow the drumbeat below. Drummers will occasionally vary the pattern slightly as they play through a song, but this is the basic beat to "Take Your Time." Notice that the snare drum (rim click) plays the repeating rhythmic pattern above.

Practice the bass drum part along with the recording. Match the bass drum rhythms exactly.

The bass guitar rhythm is similar to the bass drum rhythm. It is a 2-bar rhythmic pattern that continues throughout the tune. Practice the bass guitar part along with the recording.

Play the snare drum rhythms, which sounds the bossa nova pattern you saw at the beginning of this lesson. Hook up with the bossa nova groove.

Play the keyboard's own 2-bar rhythm. You will be playing the top note of each keyboard chord. Match the keyboard on the recording.

CHALLENGE

Try to figure out the guitar's part by ear.

BACKGROUNDS

The backgrounds to this tune can follow the keyboard part. Practice this background part along with the recording. Then create a similar background part of your own.

LESSON 27
IMPROVISATION

FORM AND ARRANGEMENT

LISTEN 39 PLAY

Listen to "Take Your Time," and try to figure out the form and arrangement by ear. Then continue with this chapter.

This tune follows a 16-bar AB form. Each phrase of the melody lasts for eight measures.

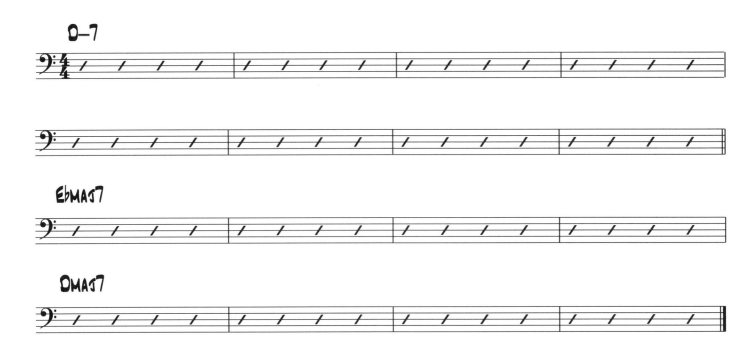

What is the arrangement on the recording? Figure it out by ear, and then check your answer against the summary at the end of this chapter.

IDEAS FOR IMPROVISING

SCALES: D PENTATONIC

For the first twelve measures of this tune (over the **D–7** and **EMAJ7** chords), we will use the *D minor pentatonic* scale to improvise. Practice this scale on your trombone.

Practice the D minor pentatonic scale throughout your entire range.

In the last four measures (over the **DMAJ7** chord), solo using notes from the *D major pentatonic scale*. Major pentatonic scales work well when improvising on major or major-7 chords. Practice this scale on your trombone.

Practice the D major pentatonic scale throughout your entire range.

CALL AND RESPONSE

1. Echo each phrase, exactly as you hear it.
2. Improvise an answer to each phrase. Imitate the sound and rhythmic feel of the phrase you hear, and use the notes from the D pentatonic scales.

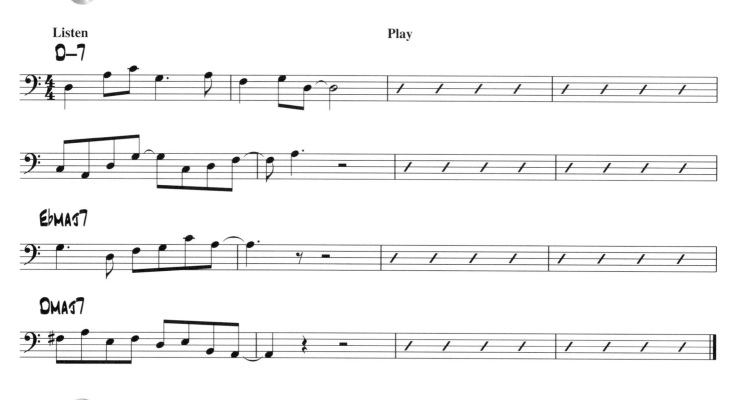

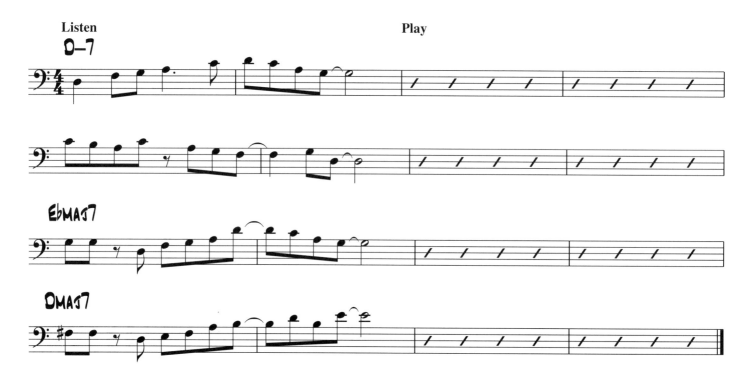

Write out some of your own ideas. Use notes from the D pentatonic scales.

𝄢

𝄢

𝄢

𝄢

𝄢

LISTEN 40 PLAY

Create a 1-chorus solo using any techniques you have learned. Memorize your solo, practice it along with the recording, and then record it.

READING

TROMBONE PART

$\frac{2}{/\!/}$ Two-measure repeat. Repeat the previously notated two measures.

Play "Take Your Time" along with the recording, and use the written part.

LISTEN **40** PLAY

TAKE YOUR TIME
TROMBONE PART
BY MATT MARVUGLIO

LEAD SHEET

Play "Take Your Time," and follow the lead sheet.

TAKE YOUR TIME

TROMBONE

BY MATT MARVUGLIO

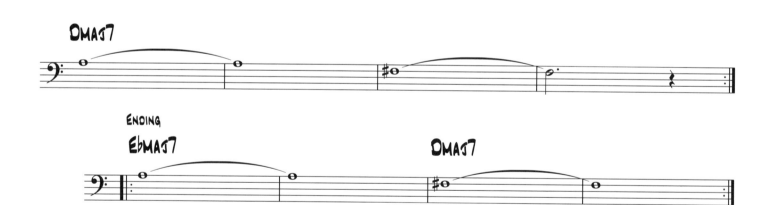

134

CHAPTER VII
DAILY PRACTICE ROUTINE

CHORD TONES AND TENSIONS

A *tension* note is an extension of a chord. The example below shows extended chord arpeggios. They are another good source of notes to use in your solos. Tensions are marked with a T below.

1. Echo each phrase, exactly as you hear it. Notice the use of tensions.
2. Improvise an answer to each phrase. Imitate the sound and rhythmic feel of the phrase you hear, and use chord tones. Try using the same tension notes as you hear on the recording.

LISTEN **43** PLAY

Write out some of your own ideas. Use notes from the D pentatonic scales and from the chord tones and tensions of D–7, FMAJ7, and DMAJ7.

LISTEN 40 PLAY

Create a 2-chorus solo using any techniques you have learned. Memorize your solo and practice it along with the recording.

SOLO PRACTICE

Practice the recorded solo along with the CD. Notice the use of long tones, chord tones, and tensions.

MEMORIZE

LISTEN **40** PLAY

Create your own solo using any of the techniques you have learned, and write it out. Practice it, memorize it, and then record yourself playing the whole tune along with the recording.

SUMMARY

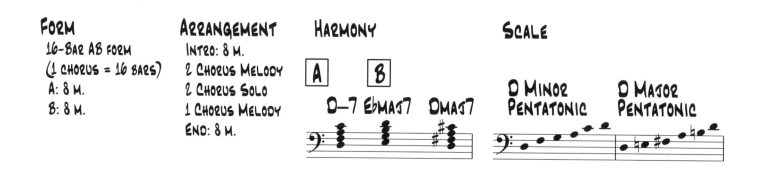

FORM	ARRANGEMENT	HARMONY	SCALE
16-BAR AB FORM	INTRO: 8 M.		
(1 CHORUS = 16 BARS)	2 CHORUS MELODY		
A: 8 M.	2 CHORUS SOLO		
B: 8 M.	1 CHORUS MELODY		
	END: 8 M.		

PLAY "TAKE YOUR TIME" WITH YOUR OWN BAND!

PLAYING STOP TIME

"Stop It" is a blues/jazz tune in which *stop time* accents the melody, like a question and answer. Stop time is very common in blues, jazz, and other styles. To hear more stop time blues, listen to Miles Davis, John Coltrane, Jim Hall, Sarah Vaughn, Bill Evans, Ella Fitzgerald, Louis Armstrong, Abbie Lincoln, Dizzy Gillespie, Charlie Parker, and trombonists Urbie Green, Curtis Fuller, Slide Hampton, Ray Anderson, George Lewis, Gary Valente, and Bill Watrous.

LESSON 29
TECHNIQUE/THEORY

Listen to the recording, and then play along with the melody. Try to match the melody. Notice that there are only three different licks.

ARTICULATION

A way to make this melody come alive is by using different articulations for the licks. The first, third, and fifth lick should all be played legato, with the notes sounding connected to each other. This is often marked with a slur.

The second lick (repeated after licks 3 and 5) is made up of five notes with alternating staccato and legato articulations.

The lick at bar 9 is also legato.

Practice the melody along with the recording, articulating these licks as shown above.

LISTEN 45 PLAY

LESSON 30
LEARNING THE GROOVE

HOOKING UP TO STOP-TIME BLUES

LISTEN **44** PLAY

Listen to "Stop It." This jazz cymbal beat is at the heart of jazz rhythm. The "spang spang-a-lang" cymbal beat is unique to jazz, and it has been its primary pattern since the 1940s. Its underlying pulse is the same as the shuffle. This pattern has accompanied Louis Armstrong, Count Basie, Miles Davis, John Coltrane, Duke Ellington, and thousands of other jazz artists.

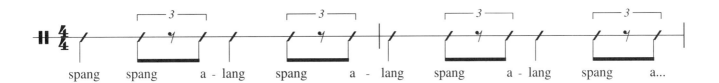

STOP TIME

In stop time, the groove is punctuated by *stop time kicks*. These are rhythmic figures, usually just one or two beats long, that punctuate the melody. That is why it is called "stop time"—the melody "stops" or rests.

Play the melody along with the recording. On this tune, the trombone plays the melody during the stop time sections. Tap the pulse with your foot, and feel the subdivisions. Hook up with the groove.

LISTEN **45** PLAY

REGULAR TIME

During the solos, the rhythm section *plays time*. The drums play a steady beat, the bass *walks* (plays steady quarter notes), and the keyboard and guitar play chords.

The guitar plays chords in a 2-measure pattern. Play the guitar part (the top note of each chord) along with the recording. Match the guitar's articulation and time feel.

The keyboard also has a repeating 2-measure pattern. Play the keyboard part (the top notes of its chords) along with the recording. Match the keyboard's articulation and time feel, and notice how it hooks up with the guitar part.

BACKGROUNDS

LISTEN **44** PLAY

At the head, play stop time kicks with the rest of the rhythm section.

At the solos, don't play a background part for the first two choruses. Come in with this first background line on the third solo chorus.

Play this second background part at the fourth solo chorus.

Practice these background parts along with the recording. Then create similar background parts of your own.

LESSON 31
IMPROVISATION

FORM AND ARRANGEMENT

Listen to "Stop It," and try to figure out the form and arrangement by ear. Check your answer against the summary at the end of this chapter.

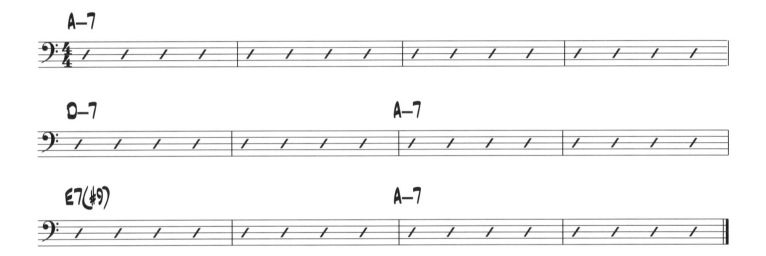

IDEAS FOR IMPROVISING

SCALES: A BLUES

Use the A blues scale to improvise on this tune.

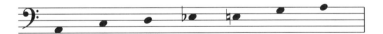

Practice the notes of the A blues scale throughout the entire range of your trombone.

Practice playing the chord tones used in this tune. Notice the extension of the **E7(#9)** chord.

The **E7(#9)** chord has a dissonance between the G-sharp and the G-natural. This color is one of the defining elements of the chord progression, and will lend a distinctive color to your solo.

Here is an example of the kind of licks you can play that make use of that dissonance.

CALL AND RESPONSE

1. Echo each phrase, exactly as you hear it.
2. Improvise an answer to each phrase. Imitate the sound and rhythmic feel of the phrase you hear. Use the A blues scale, chord tones, and tensions.

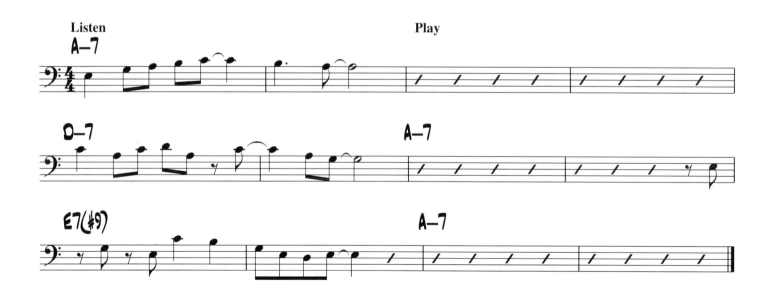

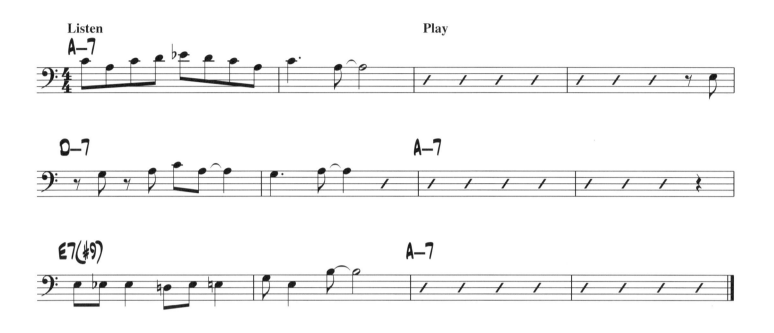

Write out some of your own ideas. Use chord tones and notes from the A blues scale.

Create a 2-chorus solo using any techniques you have learned. Memorize your solo, and practice it along with the recording.

LESSON 32
READING

TROMBONE PART

Play "Stop It" along with the recording, and read from the written trombone part.

D.C. AL ⊕

"From the beginning, and take the coda." Jump to the very first measure of the tune and play from there. When you reach the first coda symbol, skip ahead to the next coda symbol (at the end). This is similar to the "D.S. al Coda," but instead of going to a sign, go to the first measure of the tune.

STOP IT

TROMBONE PART

BY MATT MARVUGLIO

LEAD SHEET

Play "Stop It" from the lead sheet.

Stop It

TROMBONE

BY MATT MARVUGLIO

CHAPTER VIII
DAILY PRACTICE ROUTINE

CHORD TONE PRACTICE

Practice this melody, which uses chord tones and tensions of the chords to "Stop It."

CALL AND RESPONSE

1. Echo each phrase, exactly as you hear it.
2. Improvise an answer to each phrase. Use the rhythms shown and choose notes from the chord tones shown below the staff. Be sure to mix up the chord tones, rather than playing them in the order shown.

Listen   Play

Write out a few of your own ideas. Use chord tones and the A blues scale.

LISTEN 49 PLAY

Create a 2-chorus solo using any techniques you have learned. Memorize your solo, and practice it along with the recording.

SOLO PRACTICE

Practice the recorded trombone solo along with the CD.

MEMORIZE

LISTEN **49** PLAY

Create your own solo using any of the techniques you have learned, and write it out. Practice it, memorize it, and then record yourself playing the whole tune along with the recording.

SUMMARY

FORM	ARRANGEMENT	HARMONY	SCALE
12-Bar Blues (1 chorus = 12 bars)	2 Chorus Melody 4 Chorus Solo 2 Chorus Melody End: 1 m.	A–7 D–7 E7(♯9)	A Blues

PLAY "STOP IT" WITH YOUR OWN BAND!

FINAL REMARKS

Congratulations on completing the *Berklee Practice Method*. You now have a good idea of the role of the trombone in a band, and have command of the eight grooves and time feels of these tunes. The articulations and the solos that you have learned are important and useful parts of your musical vocabulary. In addition, you have tools and ideas for creating your own solos. This is a great start!

What to do next? Play along with your favorite recordings. Find recordings that you hear other musicians talking about. Learn these tunes, grooves, and solos. There is a good reason that musicians talk about certain bands, albums, or trombonists. Continue your theory, reading, and technique work. Investigate chord scales and modes. Learn all your key signatures (major and minor), scales, and chord arpeggios.

Develop your concept of what it means to play trombone. Realize how important you are as a trombonist in a band. You have a big responsibility, playing the melody, backgrounds, and improvising. It is a powerful position.

Play every day, by yourself and with others, and get the sound in your body.

Keep the beat!

—Jeff Galindo